Katsina

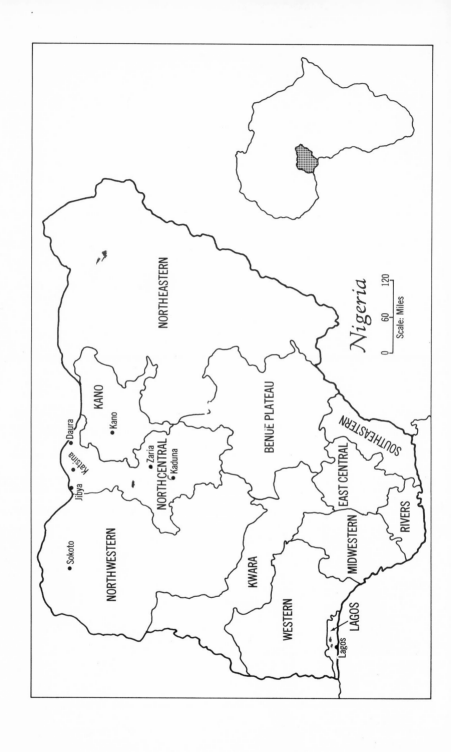

Nigeria

Scale: Miles
0   60   120

Katsina

Profile of a Nigerian City

GRETCHEN DIHOFF

PRAEGER PUBLISHERS
New York · Washington · London

To Dr. George H. Szanto

PRAEGER PUBLISHERS
111 Fourth Avenue, New York, N.Y. 10003, U.S.A.
5, Cromwell Place, London S.W.7, England

Published in the United States of America in 1970
by Praeger Publishers, Inc.

© 1970 by Praeger Publishers, Inc.

Library of Congress Catalog Card Number: 76-117473

Printed in the United States of America

Contents

Acknowledgments

That this book was ever written is due largely to Alhaji Sir Usman Nagogo, Emir of Katsina, who graciously allowed us to make our home in Katsina and to participate in its daily life.

I would also like to thank Alhaji Kabir Usman, Magagin Garin Katsina, who, with his deep knowledge and understanding of Islam, taught me much—more than I could include in this one volume. I hope that what I did use is conveyed clearly and accurately.

Mallam Ali Yusufu, N.C.E., encouraged my project of presenting his hometown to readers from other nations and gave invaluable assistance in editing the manuscript.

S. J. Hogben and A. H. M. Kirk-Greene's excellent, comprehensive book *Emirates of Northern Nigeria* greatly increased my knowledge of the history of that region, which includes Katsina.

Introduction

Katsina has been our home for two years. It has been a good home, a place we have come to like and know well. Through effort and luck, we—my husband, myself, and our two little girls, who in speech and gesture are now more Hausa than American—were able to enter into much of the lives of the people of Katsina. Friends, either by bringing us into their homes or by describing and explaining their customs, have enabled us to understand them and their neighbors. This book, then, is a story of Katsina as seen by an outsider who has had the opportunity, through close acqaintance with its people, to see their life from the inside.

Katsina

A View
of Katsina

ARRIVING BY HORSEBACK at a small rise to the north of it, we see the Hausa city of Katsina spread out in the glaring sunshine of late afternoon. Behind the walls are low, mud-brick buildings, with the tower of the Gobirau mosque rising above them. Beyond are the minarets of a new mosque. The green flag waving atop the Emir's palace signals to the people that the *Sarkin Katsina* is within. Here and there, a corrugated tin roof reflects the sun like a mirror, but the city mostly seems to be one with the land around it—little changed since Leo Africanus, one of the earliest African explorers, visited it over four hundred years ago.

Katsina is built in the style of desert cities. Now, in the last month of the rainy season, the land is not a desert.

Around the hillock, where our horses stand impatiently while we look down on the city, are fields of millet and guinea corn. Their green stalks rise high above our heads, the ears of corn offering an almost insurmountable temptation to the horses as we ride through the fields.

Farmers pass us, their short-handled hoes, *masassabi*, hooked over their shoulders. The rains will end soon; it is the busiest time of year for them. Donkeys, their mouths trapped in hemp muzzles to keep them from eating the grain around them, plod down the path, their backs laden with the first harvestings. The farmers greet us with "*barka da kilisa*," the salutation for those on horseback.

Later, on the road leading to town, we meet two old men, also on horseback, and ride a short distance with them. We experience a feeling of the camaraderie of horsemen, but any passerby could immediately see the contrast of our life styles, as evidenced by our jeans, boots, and English saddles and the old men's robes, turbans, and high, wooden Hausa saddles. They turn off the road toward their village, and, for a moment, squinting against the sunlight, we can imagine the same horsemen riding to join Fulani regiments in the jihads, the religious wars against infidels or Muslim heretics, of the eighteenth century.

We approach the city walls, but, because it is still light and we wish to continue our ride, we follow the circle of the walls. The path is narrow. On one side is the bush —scrub forest, dark and cool, tangled with thorn bushes and alive with small birds, animals, and insects. On the other side is the ravine from which the mud for the walls was taken. Water is in it now, water covered with pale green algae and lily pads; above the still water, the air hums with mosquitoes. On the far side of the ravine rise the walls. Some sections have crumbled; goats sit complacently on the ledges, formed either by rain washing the mud away or by people digging mud out to build houses.

But much of the wall is still standing—twenty feet high, five feet thick. At intervals, guava trees—in people's gardens—poke their branches over the top of the wall; sometimes houses are backed up against the wall, using it as a fourth side.

There are seven gates to Katsina. Some of them have been restored and are now graceful arches of grey cement;

Two of Katsina's Seven Gates—Kofar Sauri and Kofar Yandaka

one retains most of the original mud-brick arch. The others have crumbled into mere openings in the wall. The gates are named for the section of the town into which they lead, the destination of the road that goes away from them, or certain past district heads. Whenever the present head of one of those districts comes to Katsina, he must enter the city by the gate named for his predecessor.

The gates are Kofar Sauri, Kofar Durbi (named for the district head of Mani), Kofar Marusi (named for the district head of Dutsi), Kofar Kaura, Kofar Yandaka, Kofar Sobonwar, and Kofar Guga. Outside this last gate stands

The Signpost Outside Kofar Guga

an ambitious road sign: Gao—797 miles: Timbuctu—1,030 miles; Algiers—2,743 miles. It is a signpost to the past, as well as to distant lands—a signpost to the times when Gao and Timbuctu were the centers of great empires and to the Middle Ages, when Katsina was linked to Europe. Through this gate, Kofar Guga, from Jibya, come the desert people of the north: the Tuareg, the men of the blue veil. Their faces are half-covered by swaths of rough, indigo-dyed cloth; their bodies are robed in the same material. Only their eyes are uncovered, eyes that are dark and beautiful, almost feminine. But the swords hanging at their sides, the strong hands weathered by sandstorms belie any doubts of masculinity engendered by delicate facial features. They come on camels, on horseback, or on foot. They carry

A Tuareg Camel Train

canteens, made from calabashes and slung on a strap over their shoulders (although many have become modernized to the point where they carry water in a gallon kerosene can); knives and swords, which, although decorated, are not mere adornment; blankets and sleeping mats; and, perhaps, rolled up in the mats, food for a day or two. Often, they will be seen carrying tea kettles, another borrowing from the Western world; the spout of the tea kettles can be used easily for ritual ablutions, as well as for pouring water into the mouth as a method of drinking.

Their camels are laden with salt, mined in the desert, and dates, carried across the Sahara from the North African coast. They come to the Katsina market, just inside the Guga gate, a sprawling ten-acre plot filled with rows of

Peanuts, Millet, and Other Grains for Sale

Leather Containers for Kohl (Eye Shadow) and Perfume

stalls bearing meat, tomatoes, onions, pumpkins, corn meal, buttons, cloth, shirts, kerosene lamps, sandals, beads, perfumes, canned milk, sugar cane—the list could go on forever. Given enough time, one could find almost anything in the stalls of the market.

Children wander among the stalls, selling fried cakes that resemble doughnuts, seed cakes, peanut candy, taffy, and little animals made from cow hide decorated with feathers. At the far end of the market place is the livestock section, with herds of mournful sheep and goats in the shadow of the butcher house waiting to be sold. Vultures ring the

Goats near Market Place

walls of the abattoir, occasionally swooping down to steal a hunk of meat. Around the slaughterhouse are found the enormous horns of the Bornu cattle and hides hanging on racks.

There is much to see in the market, but only to see it would be the same as to watch a film without its sound track. The noise, even on a weekday, is a counterpoint of melody and cacophony. On Friday, market day, it rises to symphony pitch. The echo-like exchanges of greetings, the formal inquiries about the health and well-being of families, run throughout the scene as a gently rolling bass murmur.

Over this rise the shrill but still melodic cries of the hawkers. Often, a sound truck will pull up on the street that runs along the market place and loudly advertise patent medicines guaranteed to cure all ills and rejuvenate old men. Drummers—perhaps on their way to a wedding or a naming ceremony, perhaps just feeling like drumming—walk through, adding to the noise. Chickens screech and goats baa; donkeys add to the din with their metallic-sounding, unbelievable brays, not even hinted at by the feeble onomatopoeia of "hee-haw."

If anybody were making a movie of the Katsina market, he would be forced to go beyond the limits of present-day cinematography to the "smellies" of science fiction. The sights and sounds of the market can be captured on film, but the smell really *is* the market.

Open sewers, ditches alongside the streets, provide the background—by no means a stench—for all the smells of the market: the stinging, sneezy tang of red peppers, the

Okra and Peppers for Sale in the Market

unmistakable odor of peanuts, and familiar but unidentifiable aromas of spices. These aromatic odors come from the medicine stalls, where bits of dried bark, leaves, garlic, and lumps of alum and potash are displayed—the ingredients for tisanes and powders. This is a Muslim country, so only herbal medicine is displayed. In southern Nigeria, where the old "pagan" religions and juju (magic) linger, one might find in the medicine stalls dried chameleons, monkeys' paws, birds' heads, feathers, and snake skins—items that extend their powers to the foreigners who, while scoffing at them, receive, at the sight of them, an uncomfortable prickling sensation at the back of their necks.

Not that magic is entirely absent in Hausaland. Often, on a market day, a crowd will gather around a visiting snake charmer, who after exhibiting his power over cobras and pythons, will briskly sell "medicine" that he claims will protect the wearer from snake bites. These are usually small leather pouches that contain amulets bearing a passage from the Koran and, for good measure, a sprinkling of special dust. The pouches are sewn shut, and he who opens one—out of curiosity or doubt—does so at his own risk. Snake charmers are not the only people who dispense charms. There are charms guaranteeing success at gambling, winning at sports, and safety on the roads. The fact that these last can be seen still dangling from the rear-view mirrors of overturned buses does not seem to lessen people's faith in their efficacy.

The smells of spices are not the most long-lingering odors in the market. The smell of wood smoke pervades the market, arising from the areas where men are beginning to roast *tsire:* cubes of lamb or goat meat, skewered on sticks stuck in the ground around a hot fire. The meat, first coated with ground red pepper, has shocked more than one newcomer to Nigerian food.

Tsire, Cubes of Lamb or Goat Meat,
Being Prepared in the Market

Depending on the season, aisles of the open-air market
will be perfumed by lemons, oranges, guavas, and mangoes.
Elsewhere, the leather-workers' stalls have their own dis-
tinctive odor, which mingles with the dusty smell from
blankets hanging for sale nearby. Sweet, pungent, fragrant,
nauseating—nothing smells quite like a Nigerian market.

A Shop in Town

The streets that lead away from the market run off at odd angles and are congested with small shops. Beds are ranged in front of one shop, chicken wire and lumber are piled before another. Canned goods and other groceries line the shelves inside many of the tiny one-room shops, where Japanese tuna leans against Australian pears and American canned corn. But no shop is entirely specialized. A shop selling radios, irons, flashlights, and other electric items may also have a few cans of dried milk and several boxes of cookies on the shelves. A grocery store may display tea kettles and jerseys.

Many of the articles are Nigerian-made, including handicrafts and products of the country's expanding industry. The imports come from such far-flung parts of the world as England, the United States, Greece, and Iceland. One wonders if the factory worker in Reykjavik ever suspects that the fish he is processing might end up in an African pepper stew.

Running at right angles to the market road is the most commercial street in the town. It leads out to the Kaura gate, the road to Kano; it is lined with gas stations catering

One of Katsina's Many Service Stations

to the heavy truck traffic. There is no competition for the most advantageous corner; all stations are in a row, right next to one another. This abundance of stations proves convenient; because Katsina is at the far end of the tanker route, a particular station is often short of gasoline. If Mobil is out, the attendant cheerfully waves the customer on to Shell, where he may be cheerfully waved on to Texaco.

On this road is the truck park, where trucks, carrying peanuts and other produce to other parts of Nigeria, collect passengers. The travelers sit—rather uncomfortably and dangerously—atop the cargo. For shorter journeys, there are small trucks, with brightly painted wooden frames built onto their bodies. These are crammed to the brim with people and their baggage—chickens, cooking pots, and bundles of personal belongings. Then a few more people are crowded in, and the trip begins. There is no set schedule for arrivals and departures; the trucks set off when they have enough passengers.

On this road, also, are the post office and the telegraph office, the public adult-education building, and the Coca-Cola and Sprite distributor. The tire repairmen—called vulcanizers—have their workshops, marked by piles of old tires, set up conveniently near the gas stations. The mechanics are also situated on this street, their establishments advertised by rusted, discarded engine parts or, occasionally, by the body of a car, with its re-usable parts stripped away.

Near the town wall are the Local Authority police barracks and the stables, where horses, used for both police duty and polo, are kept. There, the Emir's fife and drum band can be heard practicing in the afternoon. At night, far different music is heard farther down the road—practically in the shadow of the wall—at the local hotel. On week nights, it might only be records or a *goge*, a one-string calabash violin, accompanied by drums; on weekends, big bands often come from Zaria or Kano, and play high life, the Cha-Cha, and Beatles' songs.

Running at an angle between these two main streets—the market and Kano roads—is a small street leading to a crumbled gate, the Yandaka gate, where Lugard, the British colonial governor, entered Katsina in 1903, when it came under British rule. The street is very narrow, flanked on either side by houses. Although the main streets may carry

Plaque at the Yandaka Gate

most of the commercial enterprises in Katsina, this small street—which leads to an insignificant gate, which leads, in turn, to little but the polo field and, beyond that, to farm paths—is the fullest and liveliest in Katsina.

The crowded market, with a jumble of shops around it, or the bustle of the Kano road does not begin to give an idea of the size and complexity of Katsina life.

Katsina is a Hausa town, a Muslim town, where women

are kept secluded in purdah. Actual living quarters are hidden from casual eyes, behind walls and outer reception rooms. Streets that seem to hold only a row of shops or drab, almost unused-looking houses, actually mask a teeming maze of humanity, animals, gardens, schools, mosques, and perhaps, tiny factories pressing peanut oil or smithing silver.

On *Hainyar Gidan Yari* (Prison Street), the small street that leads to the Yandaka gate, life seems to spill out into the open. Near the center of town is the prison itself, a complex of high stone walls. From here, each day, details of prisoners with guards go out to cut grass along the roads, help repair streets, work on farms, or gather firewood for the prison kitchens.

Farther down the street are the millet grinders, with their mills always whirring and women and children clustered around, waiting for their sacks of flour. Then there are the dye pits, the *marina*, where homespun thread is dipped into holes in the ground filled with indigo dye.

Some important event is always going on. Drummers are always beating in front of one house or another for weddings, naming ceremonies, simple parties celebrating good harvests, school exams passed, or just from an excess of good spirits.

Few shops are readily noticeable; here, as elsewhere in Nigeria, most shops are carried on the heads of vendors. Girls sell millet porridge; men hawk buns and tea—they carry huge trays of rolls, sugar cubes, and cans of evaporated milk on their heads and hold enormous tea kettles with charcoal braziers wired underneath. Fruit, fried cakes, cigarettes, matches, kola nuts, peanuts, chickens—no street in Katsina, indeed, in all of Nigeria, is *not* commercial. Everyone sells something.

To ears used to the machine noises of American cities,

A Tea and Bun Vendor

the din of a Katsina street sounds peculiar. It is loud, but it is the loudness of human voices and fits comfortably within the limits of human hearing. The Hausa is dignified and reserved when viewed in most situations, but seen, so to speak, in his own backyard, he never seems to stop talking. Children are noisy anywhere, but, when Hausa children see a foreigner driving down their street, they feel compelled to shout, *"Bature!"* ("White man!"). It does not matter if the same person has driven down their street twice a day for years; the children always want to remark on the sight —at the top of their lungs. The shawls of the women, which decorously cover their faces as they walk among strangers, do not seem to diminish the amplitude of their voices as they gossip.

An unknown language heard spoken on all sides always seems musical. All one really hears is sound, which the brain does not decode into meaning. Whether one understands it or not, Hausa, with a phonology based on tones, is always musical. The voices, the drums beating intricate rhythms, the steady whir of the grinding machines, the thump of pestles pounding guinea corn in giant mortars combine in the evensong of a Hausa town.

The Kano road receives the outside world through its trucks and cars, its gasoline tankers, and its delivery van, which carries copies of the *New Nigerian Newspaper*. But the road running at right angles to it, out toward the Durbi gate, on the edge of ancient Katsina, is the place where the outside world has taken residence.

The two cinemas are on this road; every night hundreds of people watch the stylized adventures of Indian stars imitating Sean Connery playing James Bond and Doris Day playing one of her typical roles.

It is outside the old walls themselves, however, separated by distance and attitude from the indigenous life of Katsina, that the representatives of the Western world have built their strongholds—the bank, aloof and white-painted; GBO, a wholesale store, largely patronized for its beer; the mission bookstore, which sells Christmas cards to Muslims; the cold store, a grocery store much like those in town, except that it boasts two refrigerators, which hold butter, cheese, bacon, and frozen fish to satisfy the hungers of homesick expatriates.

Just beyond the cold store is a traffic circle, with roads spinning off to the airport (a tiny airstrip used when VIP's visit) and the GRA, the Government Residential Area—a holdover from colonial days, when the administrators would not deign to live amidst the sounds and smells of the city. Now the houses are inhabited by the town's two doctors, teachers from the secondary school and the men's and women's teachers' colleges, engineers, and a few stray agricultural experts.

Years ago, Hausa rulers subtly defied the inroads of British domination and Western culture: The houses they built for the colonial officials were in the traditional style,

Governmental Residence Constructed in Traditional Hausa Style

with thick mud walls and flat roofs. Inside, to be sure, they were modern, with plumbing and kitchens to satisfy any Western housewife, but, in appearance, they merged with the land and the people around them. For many reasons— among them, the cost and difficulty of maintenance and the stubborn resistance of expatriates—the houses have been abandoned and stand, empty and weatherworn, among the new prefab and concrete structures.

In the center of Katsina is a walled quarter, the Emir's palace. The part containing his residence, gardens, guest house, and stables is called *chikin gida* (within the house). The rest of his quarter contains the offices of his secretary, meeting rooms for district councils, and the homes of the Emir's whole entourage, over a thousand people.

Upon entering the gates of the palace compound, one might feel as if he had been transported to the world of the *Thousand and One Nights,* with turbaned guards and jasmine-scented gardens. Or, he might encounter the twentieth-century world, for instance, a meeting of district heads discussing means of conveying 2,000 tons of peanuts to Lagos, for shipment to the peanut butter factories of the world.

It is evening; the sun is low on the horizon, and, from the minaret, the call is sounded for evening prayer. Women walk to the well near the Kofar Sauri, the last gate still standing unbroken. It is the final week of the rainy season. Already the stream running beside the road is narrow; soon it will disappear. Women draw water to fill their clay jugs, just as they have done for centuries, except that now, instead of using a leather or calabash bucket, they may use one made out of rubber from an inner tube.

This scene at the well captures the essence of Katsina and of the greater part of Nigeria; it is a place between— between the desert and the jungle, between ancient traditions and industrialization. Katsina is a city that must decide —before the decision is made for it—where it is going and how it will get there.

2

The People of Katsina

KATSINA IS ITS PEOPLE: the old Fulani women walking slowly into town, with homespun, indigo-dyed wrappers pulled around their thin bodies, calabashes of fermented milk balanced on their heads; the *malamai*, with white robes and small grey beards, carrying leather bags, which contain copies of the Koran; the Yoruba students from the nursing school, walking toward the hospital in their crisp white uniforms and stylish high-heeled sandals; the grease- and carbon-smeared mechanics at the service stations.

Katsina is a small city, with a population of about sixty thousand. The Hausa form the majority; the rest includes a few thousand Yoruba from the southern part of Nigeria, some Tiv, members of several minor ethnic groups from the middle belt, Fulani—the majority settled and thoroughly mixed with the Hausa, the rest (the bush, or cow, Fulani) nomadic people who wander through Katsina, following their herds to the grasslands, selling milk or cattle—and the Tuareg, the people of the desert, who come mostly during the dry season, on camels bearing salt.

Until the middle of 1966, a large Ibo population lived in Katsina, whose number at least equaled that of the Yoruba group. In the riots that preceded the second Nigerian *coup d'état*, in July, 1966, a number of Ibo were killed; the remainder fled to the southeast from Katsina and the rest of northern Nigeria. During 1969, Ibo have returned to the larger cities of the north and will probably return eventually to the smaller cities such as Katsina.

Characteristics of appearance and personality are ascribed to the members of Nigerian ethnic groups by other groups and by themselves in much the same manner as members of national groups in America are popularly stereotyped. The Yoruba are considered fun-loving, excitable, and hustling. The Tiv are thought to be strong and quick-tempered —not people with whom to pick a fight. The Hausa are thought of as dignified and proper and as shrewd traders. The Tuareg and bush Fulani are supposed to be equally dignified, but they are considered unsophisticated and bumbling by townspeople because they are nomadic. The Ibo, generally better educated in the Western sense than most of their Hausa neighbors, appeared arrogant and were known for their business acumen.

The capsule characterization of the Tuareg by popular opinion may be apt. When forced to deal with certain aspects of modern life, the Tuareg is often helpless. Once, for example, three Tuareg were running down the road leading to the Durbi gate. Their caravan had started without them, and they were trying to catch up with it before it left town.

Old Fulani Women Carrying Calabashes

We stopped and offered them a lift in our Volkswagen. For several minutes, indescribable confusion reigned while the men clambered in and sat on the floor of the back seat, getting their swords tangled in legs and robes and their turbans knocked askew. They had no conception of how to enter a car and sit on the seats.

Before laughing too mercilessly at the thought of this awkward spectacle, however, one should try mounting a camel. This the Tuareg does without any effort by the time he is a few years old.

A Tuareg Astride His Camel

The camel kneels obediently—if an experienced camel driver tells it to do so—and the rider scrambles into the saddle. This is like a high-backed chair, with an equally high, thinner piece in front. It is wooden, sometimes padded with cloth or leather, and attached to the camel by a single cinch about five inches wide. When seated more or less comfortably on this precarious perch, with one foot planted firmly on the nape of the camel's elongated neck, one gives the command to rise—or asks the driver to address the

Two Tuareg Passing Through Katsina

camel. The animal straightens its hind legs first, with its front knees still on the ground. This pitches saddle and rider forward at a dizzy angle, while raising them about six feet off the ground. Just when it seems impossible to defy gravity any longer, the camel straightens its front legs, pitching the saddle and rider sharply back. Then the rider is reasonably level, perched seven or eight feet above the ground and wobbling from side to side and front to back, as the camel plods along. For the Westerner, the whole operation is almost impossible to complete without terrified shrieks or, at least, sharp intakes of breath. The Tuareg does not indulge in such hysteria.

Two Tuareg Men

A self-contained people, they have absorbed little of the Westernized culture around them, beyond an occasional tea kettle or kerosene can. They seldom wear Western clothes, preferring the voluminous robes that have protected them from the desert sun for generations. Their clothes— called *riga* in Hausa—are similar in style to those worn throughout Nigeria and most of West Africa: cotton trousers, cut very wide through the legs and bound to the waist with a drawstring; over this, a robe that is cut from a huge rectangle of cloth, folded in half crosswise, with a keyhole opening on the fold for the head and the sides stitched together at the bottom. The great expanse of sleeve is rolled up into large folds over the shoulders. On one or both arms is a bracelet carved from black soapstone and worn over the biceps. Around the neck or waist is a *laya*, a leather thong from which dangle several small leather pouches, which contain special powders or passages from the Koran; charms against disease, accident, and snakebite; and charms for luck and strength. On the feet are handmade sandals, either made of leather or fashioned out of rubber cut from worn-out tires. The head is covered by a turban, either white or dark blue, depending on the social status; a noble —rank is based on inherited position and personal wealth— wears blue, and a commoner wears white. Part of the turban hangs down the side of the face and can be drawn across the mouth and chin like a veil.

The Tuareg is one of the Berber peoples who roam the Sahara. In Katsina, one sees very few, if any, Tuareg women, although there are often some in the big market at Jibya, thirty miles north, on the Niger Republic border. Newcomers, and even people used to the sight, will often stare at the Tuareg passing by on their camels or walking disdainfully through the market. They carry an air of mystery —with their silent walk, their half-hidden faces, and their sense of self-sufficiency. They ignore the stares.

Bush Fulani, however, return the stares, and they preen themselves when being curiously scrutinized. First sight of a Fulani may come in the evening while one is driving toward Katsina. A line of women walking along the side of the road catches one's attention. The mind immediately associates the unknown with the known: Indians. High cheekbones; narrow, sometimes hooked noses; long hair plaited into two braids and fastened with twists of gold thread— they do, indeed, resemble, at first glance, American Indians. The same women, when seen at close range—perhaps sit-

ting in the market place with their calabashes of milk—are
even more striking. In their ears are heavy earrings—six or
seven huge silver hoops or long, dangling baubles made
from old coins. They may also be wearing heavy necklaces
of old coins. Often, these include French, Belgian, English,
or other European coins dating from the eighteenth and
nineteenth centuries.

Young Fulani women seem almost universally attractive
—perhaps this is so because one is refreshed by the sight of
any young women in a Muslim town—a place where women
are kept locked in their homes during their attractive years.

Fulani Girl

Fulani girls wear a short, heavily embroidered, midriff
blouse and bright-colored wrappers. Older women usually
wear a dark blue wrapper tied over the chest. Although
they no longer dress coquettishly once their figures have
deteriorated (through childbirth and nursing), older Fulani
women still wear jewelry—so much of it that the old
women carrying milk or firewood seem as much bowed by
the weight of their necklaces and earrings as they do by
the burdens on their heads.

Both men and women use cosmetics—dark blue kohl

eye shadow, rouge, lipstick, nail polish, powder, and perfume. A Fulani man might wear several kinds of clothes—an embroidered tunic of roughly woven cotton or a more heavily embroidered tunic of finer cotton, with enormously

Another Fulani Girl

billowing, embroidered trousers extending to mid-calf, fitting tightly at the cuff. When he is walking with the cattle, he often will wear an apron-like garment of leather over ragged shorts or trousers.

A Westerner might get a false impression of a Fulani man, seeing him seated by the side of the road, wearing his flared tunic, deftly darkening his eyebrows with a piece of

Fulani Man

charcoal or paring his long, reddened fingernails. The knife
he is using for his nails, however, should allay any suspicion
of femininity. Its blade is meant for business, whether for
paring fingernails, slaughtering cattle, or injuring a man. If
a Fulani man removes his peacock tunic, the scars on his
back bear eloquent evidence of another side of his nature.

When a Fulani male reaches puberty, he must undergo a beating ceremony. At the end of the rainy season—the harvest time—when the herdsmen begin to move south in their search for grass for their cattle, young men of the Fulani community gather together, each with two friends who have already gone through the ceremony.

The sun is hot overhead. In the village, where the temporary lean-tos of the Fulani are found on one side and the solider mud huts of the Hausa farmers on the other, drums beat a deep-bass rhythm. A crowd encircles an open field. A young man stands in the circle, bare-chested, his arms

Fulani Beating Ceremony

hooked over a stick that rests across his shoulders, his bare back exposed and vulnerable. He challenges the young men

Marks of Fulani Manhood

from the other villages. Behind him, one of his friends is encouraging him. Another friend, sitting on the ground before him, is singing his praises enthusiastically.

Finally, someone answers his challenge. The young man carries a whip, cut from a tree whose wood is noted for its quality of staying green and supple long after it has been cut. Perhaps he has a locally known substance on it to make the welts more painful. But the boy to be beaten has already drunk a special potion and is wearing charms on a leather thong around his waist.

The beater approaches. There is no enmity or anger between the two boys. This is only a ceremony, real and painful though it is. The beater declares the number of strokes he will give—he bases his decision not on the stamina of the boy he is about to beat but rather, according to the number he knows he himself can withstand, for the beating will be reciprocated.

In the beginning, the boy being beaten must not flinch or cry out. Blood can spurt from welts raised on his bare back, but the young man being tested wears a fixed smile. Behind him, one friend encourages him; before him, another praises him. Perhaps even more courage is elicited by the murmur of praise from the young Fulani women in the circle, for, if he exhibits bravery, the young man will be able to marry from among the most beautiful. He continues to smile.

To the Westerner, the Tiv present no conflict of outer appearance and inner character. Both men and women are tall, broad-shouldered, and heavy. The physical education teacher at Katsina Teachers' College is a Tiv. When he first came, he overwhelmed the students—heretofore somewhat lackadaisical when it came to sports and athletics—with his drive and endurance, and the fact that he expected them to match his own energy.

The Yoruba represent such a large segment of the population of Katsina, that, while they are usually as easily recognizable as Tuareg or Fulani, they are hard to describe with generalities. A girl seen in Katsina in modern Western dress is most likely to be a Yoruba, as is true of a girl working in a shop, a nurse at the hospital—male or female—and a clerk at the post office.

Dupe, a Yoruba, works in the cold store. She comes from Ilorin Province, the part of Yorubaland that reaches into what used to be the Northern Region. Most of the Yoruba in Katsina are from that region; many are Muslim and, thus, are used to the Katsina pattern of life even before they come there. Dupe is Christian and attends the services every

Sunday in the mission building across from the mission book store. She has a Christian name, Esther, but most people call her Dupe.

Tall and well built, she is popular with her customers, but none of them would marry her. She is too modern, too immodest. Nor would she marry any of these Hausa men, because she is too independent to want to live the subjugated life that Hausa women consider normal. She has completed primary school and four years of secondary school, and is continuing her studies through a correspondence school, hoping to get her school certificate.

Like most Yoruba girls, she alternates between traditional wrappers and blouses and modern short-skirted dresses; between bare feet and fancy sandals. Most of the time her hair is plaited into several braids, in patterns that are tradi-

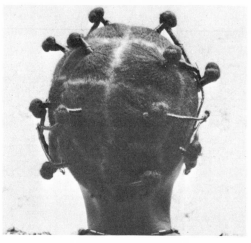

One Style of Hair-Plaiting

tional and quite attractive. She cannot do the plaiting herself; Funmilayo, her best friend, comes to plait her hair for her once a week, during the two-hour break from noon to 2 P.M. when the store is closed. Dupe does Funmilayo's hair the day after her hair has been plaited. The children of Joseph, the manager of the mission book store, come to watch, giggling if Dupe complains that Funmilayo is pulling her hair.

Dupe ranks in the middle of the social scale of the Yoruba community in Katsina. Above her are the provincial police officer, the postmaster, and the principal of the teachers' college. But social position means little to the Yoruba—Dupe treats them all alike. (Before the 1966 riots, Ibo held many of the positions Yoruba now fill in the post office, bank, municipal administration, shops, and businesses.)

The Yoruba are the largest minority group in Katsina. The expatriates constitute the second largest; they are grouped together merely because they are foreigners. Little else is similar among them. Some have lived in Katsina for many years and do not foresee leaving. The water engineer, an Anglo-Arab, has been there for fourteen years, and two Lebanese, managing the cinemas and some cloth shops, are equally permanently settled in the community. The rest are usually on tours of one or two years. Some extend their contracts, some leave as soon as they can, some are transferred at the whim of the government agency or company that employs them. They include the two doctors at the hospital—at the moment, an Egyptian and a Sudanese—a few engineers attached to the Ministry of Works, the department that deals with road building, plumbing, and electrical repairs; one or two U.S. Agency for International Development (U.S. AID) agricultural agents; and the rest teachers in one of the three secondary schools—a mixed group of Americans (Peace Corps, U.S. AID, and private contract), British, Canadians, Indians, Pakistanis, Ceylonese, Danish, and Dutch.

The expatriates have a wide range of rapport with the people of Katsina. Some consider it enough to have to cope with the climate without having to deal with the people. Others, who have not yet fully realized Nigeria's independence, talk about "them" and the "natives." Still others have become a part of Katsina and do not feel that when March comes, and most of the expatriates go on home leave, "there's no one left in town."

Despite the varied minority groups of Katsina's population, it is, and always has been, a Hausa town. The Hausa are easy to stereotype; they are usually serious, tall, and stately. But they often, and disconcertingly, elude such easy stereotyping. The chief nurse at the hospital, a tall, handsome man, is not at all given to dignity, bouncing from ward to ward with ceaseless energy, joking and smiling. He is also as willing as any American father to dandle his children on his lap, absent-mindedly holding a bottle for the baby while inspecting the older one's broken doll.

Ten or fifteen white-robed dignitaries—district heads, who are advisers to the Emir—calmly inspect the town zoo. While they are peering into the snake pit, watching pythons writhing below, one stately, grey-bearded gentleman stoops and runs a twig along the ankle of a colleague, making him jump with terror, thinking that a snake has just brushed his leg.

But the stereotyped descriptions are for the most part true. Malama Mai Kwai, the egg woman (*mai*—owner of; *kwai*—eggs), a farmer's wife who raises a dozen or so chickens and guinea hens, comes to the door once or twice a week, her basin of eggs balanced on her head. She squats on the porch to test her eggs in a bucket of water (bad eggs float); she accepts the greetings of the gardener and passersby; she protests the discarding of certain eggs, retests them; she is completely in control of the situation. Nothing disturbs her.

Ali, a deaf-mute beggar, appears from time to time at the

cold store, at the post office, and at the gas station. He is, compared with the other boys who beg (as is required by their Koranic school), usually clean and reasonably well dressed. He has his own clientele, and he diligently watches the cars, opens the doors, and drives off any stray beggars who try to infringe on his territory. He disappears for days or weeks at a time. One is not really terribly surprised to meet him in the main square of Maradi, a town sixty miles away in the Niger Republic. Once, for his own reasons— perhaps only wanderlust—he passed through both the Nigerian and the Niger border stations, through two more Niger police checks on the road from the border to Maradi, stayed there long enough to beg enough money to return to Katsina—all with a calm air of self-sufficiency.

3

History

KATSINA WAS ONE of the seven original Hausa states, the Hausa Bakwai, which came into being in the eleventh century. By no means a unified nation, they were a collection of city-states bound by a common culture and language, squabbling among themselves and fighting invasions from the bigger nations around them—the Songhai Empire, to the north and west, and the Kanem-Bornu Empire, to the east. Katsina itself was overrun several times and, throughout its early history, paid tribute to either Songhai or Bornu.

This is the legend of the origin of the Hausa states:

Bayajida, one of the sons of the King of Baghdad, quarreled with his father and fled into exile. After many months of wandering, he came to Daura, a town about sixty miles east of Katsina, then ruled by one of a long line of queens.

It was night when he arrived in the town, and the road had been long and dusty. He stopped at a house and asked an old woman there for water. She told him that no water was to be had in the town. When he demanded an explanation, she replied that a sacred snake lived in the town well, and it only allowed the townspeople to draw water on Fridays. This had been going on for many years, and no one had ever been able to kill the snake.

Bayajida then left the old woman and made his way, through the dark streets of Daura, to the well. He lowered a bucket over the side, the creak of the rope echoing loud in the silent street. The serpent, hearing the sound, put its head out of the well to see who dared to violate its territory. Bayajida was ready with his sword and cut off the snake's head with a single stroke. He then drew water and drank thirstily. Then he left, carrying the snake's head with him.

The next day was Friday, and the people of the town came to draw water. To their amazement, they discovered the headless body of the great snake lying beside the well. The news quickly reached the Queen, and she asked who had succeeded in killing the snake. Many immediately claimed that they had done so. The Queen ordered that the snake's head be brought as proof.

In all the years the snake had been in the well, no one had really seen it. No one had dared to look upon it. Many stories had thus sprung up about its appearance. Men came before the Queen bearing all sorts of strange heads—of horses, goats, and cats. Finally Bayajida appeared, holding up the snake's head. The Queen knew when she saw it that this was the true head of the snake, and she dismissed the impostors with their bizarre trophies. Bayajida claimed, as his reward, marriage to the Queen. After the wedding, he settled down to rule the kingdom. Their son had seven sons, who set out to found and rule the seven original Hausa states: Daura, Katsina, Kano, Rano, Gobir, Zaria, and Biram.

Over the main gate of the walls of Daura is the town emblem, a coiled cobra, its hood spread menacingly, a sword

The Gate at Daura

plunged through its head. Daura, today, is a quiet, dusty
town in the backwater of Nigerian development. But it is
proud of its place in Hausa history. Inside the Emir's palace
rests a jeweled sword, reputed to be the sword of Bayajida.
Signs in the town point the way to a square near the palace.
Here is the well of the legend; it looks much like any of
the thousands of wells to be found in this arid savannah

The Well at Daura Where, According to Legend, Bayajida Slew the
Snake

region of Nigeria. Any one of them could be one year or a
thousand year's old—their construction is a traditional art.

Across the mouth of the Daura well are the heavy, wooden
cylinders used to support the bucket ropes. Nearly eight
inches in diameter and made of hard wood, they are entirely
worn through in several places by the friction of the count-
less ropes that have been used to lower and raise buckets.

Did the banished prince of Baghdad once stand where

we can stand today? Did he look over the edge of this well at the sinuous body of a snake that had held a city in terror for years? There is little to substantiate the story—to prove that this is really the same well or that the sword in the palace is really the sword Bayajida used.

Some basic facts lend credence to the story. Cobras do live in wells, and many a well has been abandoned because of the presence of a snake in its depths. Walwyn, in his *History of Daura*, suggests that the legend is symbolic even if based on a true incident. The killing of the snake would represent the conversion of the people from pagan worship —the sacred snake—to Islam, and Bayajida's assumption of power, the change from a matriarchal system to a patriarchal one. It is interesting to note that Bayajida took the title of *Makassarki* (Killer of Sarki), for the name of the snake was Sarki. This, in time, was shortened to *Sarki*, the Hausa word for "emir."

According to legend and available histories, the first king of Katsina was Kumayo, the grandson of Bayajida and the Queen of Daura. He did not rule in what is now the city of Katsina, but in a place called Durbi, about eight miles from Katsina on the Daura road. The Durbi gate opens on to this road.

The place is now called Durbi ta Kusheyi, Durbi—the place of graves—and is marked by a small historical-society sign pointing off the main road, down a narrow dirt track. The track crosses a stream bed and can only be negotiated by a car from September to May, when the stream is dry. Three miles from the main road there is another sign, noting the discovery of the tombs by a British administrator in the 1920's.

Farmers working in the guinea-corn fields succumb to curiosity and come near our car. Where are the tombs? There is much speculation and discussion. Then, one man comes forward. One of the tombs is in his field; he will show us the way.

Even though one remembers that the kings who are buried in this land ruled over eight hundred years ago, it is hard to imagine that this area was once the capital of a kingdom. In the distance, across the flat fields, a small village is visible, but the dwellings and palace of Durbi have long been part of the earth on which they were built. Little that man builds can withstand the wind and sun of northern Nigeria, once it has been abandoned by him.

The fields are hot in the midmorning sun, the ground rough and hard underfoot. Men and children look up from their hoeing, stare for a moment at the strange procession, then return to their work.

Suddenly the tomb is before us—a huge mound of earth

Signpost at the Durbi Tombs

covered with grass and small trees. But for the uniform flatness of the fields around it, it might be a natural hill, not a burial mound. Here, one sights no little historical-society sign. None of the farmers know who was buried here or what remains of the body and of the treasures and artifacts buried with it. Perhaps they were taken away to museums, perhaps they were too trivial to bother with.

There are seven tombs in all. The next one is a mile or two away—the farmer gestures vaguely toward the horizon. Although there is a sense of history here, there is little to see. Eight hundred years have all but erased the evidence that this was once the center of the Kingdom of Katsina.

Five generations ruled at Durbi, over a time span of 150 years. The last of the dynasty was Sanau, who was overcome, legends tell us, by trickery. Sanau was famous for his wrestling and was protected against harm by a certain charm which he always wore. Another wrestler, named Korau, came to visit, and persuaded Sanau's wife to steal the charm while her husband was sleeping. The next morning Korau challenged the King to a wrestling match. The King was bound by honor to accept the challenge, but without his charm he could not overcome Korau's strength and was thrown to the ground. Korau stabbed him to death and took over the kingdom.

Again, it is not certain to what extent this story is legend and to what extent fact. A sword, reputed to be the sword of Korau, is still among the state treasures of Katsina; the Emir carries it in the processions during Sallah, Muslim festivals celebrated in December and February. The blade does date from the thirteenth century and carries the inscription, "Help cometh from God and victory is nigh; so announce glad tidings to the faithful, O Muhammad!" (English translation from the Arabic).

Although Muslim, many of the customs of the people and rulers of Katsina date back to earlier, pagan times. The strength and vigor of the King was believed to affect the fertility of the fields and the abundance of the harvest. When the old king became ill or showed signs of weakening, it was believed better for the kingdom that he die. According to the old chronicles of Katsina, it was the duty of the court official who bore the title of *karyagiwa*, (elephant-slayer), to strangle the King when the latter appeared about to die. Korau would then seem to have been working within the traditional framework. If a King was not strong enough to withstand challengers, he did not deserve the kingship. Korau's succession was accepted without any great dissent.

Traditionally, after the new King had been chosen, a black ox was slaughtered over him so that he was drenched in the blood. The ox was then skinned, and the hide was used to wrap the body of the old King. As the body was carried through town to the burial ground, the townspeople beat on it, shouting, "Forget! Forget!" The old King had been an integral part of the people's lives, closely associated with their work, their crops, their prosperity. When he died and a new attachment had to be made, no sentimental reverence, no lingering grief could be allowed.

Pagan customs such as these existed alongside the growing acceptance of Islam. The first truly Muslim ruler did not take power until 1492. From the fifteenth to the eighteenth century, there was a long period of war and fear of war, as the kingdoms throughout this part of Africa rose and fell, with nations established and re-established, much as was happening in Europe during the same period.

Katsina came under the influence of Mali, of Songhai, and of the Bornu Empire to the east and was subject to raids from the neighboring Hausa states of Kano and Gobir—and, in its turn, raided those states when it could. Trade continued, somewhat diminished by the hazards that warfare imposed on caravan routes but enhanced by the far-flung contacts of successive invasions. The Hausa states, Katsina and Kano in particular, acted as middlemen for those bearing the riches from across the desert—salt from the mines at Taghaza, various products from Europe, and gold and spices from the rain forest to the south.

During the times of respite from foreign invasions, Katsina and the other six Hausa states continued their internecine struggles. Early in the sixteenth century, a remarkable woman became queen of Zaria, then called Zazzau, to the south of Katsina. This was Amina, whose sister Zaria gave the modern name to the Emirate. Amina was power hungry and bellicose. She led her troops against the other Hausa states and conquered them. Then she pushed south as far as the Benue River. It was her custom to have a walled encampment built wherever she and her troops stopped. The old walls of all towns are still called *ganuwar Amina* (Amina's walls)—whether or not she had them built.

The walls of Katsina are still standing almost intact around the city, despite four centuries of wind and rain. This is partly due to their thickness—over five feet—and partly due to the materials of construction. The mud was mixed with dried grass. Then cattle were driven to the building site and slaughtered to provide food for the workers. The blood was mixed into the building mud, which was then shaped into bricks for the wall. The mud had been dug from around the perimeter of the wall, thus creating, in effect, a wall and moat when the rains fell.

The Gobirau mosque did not fare as well as the walls, and all that now remains is a mud column protected by a tower, also made of mud bricks. The original mosque was built in the seventeenth century; the meager remnant is still

The Gobirau Mosque

preserved, partly because of the remarkable story of its beginning. When the leaders of the town decided to build a mosque, there was some dispute over the site. It had to face east, but no one could agree which direction *was* east. Finally a *waliyi*, a saint or holy man, settled the argument by driving his staff into the ground and asking the Emir and his council to look over the top of it. To their amazement they could see the holy city of Mecca. That, naturally, was the way the mosque was oriented.

The uncertainty over the direction of the mosque illustrates a problem that Katsina had at this time, a problem that was carried over into the nineteenth century, to be settled only by war. The citizens of Katsina were more sincerely and intensely Muslim than were the kings and ruling classes. Although the rule by Muslim kings of Katsina had been initiated at the end of the fifteenth century, the dynasty was still the lineage of Korau, who had won his title by magic. Old traditions and customs were retained, despite discrepancies with Islam. The Hausa accepted these discrepancies. The Fulani did not.

Since the beginning of the sixteenth century, the Fulani people had been spreading over much of this area. No one knows where it came from. Some believe it to be one of the lost tribes of Israel; others believe its members are descendants of Berbers, who were related to the Tuareg. Still another legend recounts that an Arab from Saudi Arabia came to a town on the Niger and married a woman of the town. He had four sons, and shortly after the birth of the last one, he left, never to return. The children spoke among themselves a language no one had ever heard before—Fulani—and from them descended the extensive tribe. This tale is part of the folklore in many parts of Nigeria.

The Fulani were, traditionally, nomadic herders, but, during the seventeenth and eighteenth centuries, many were converted to Islam. They settled in towns, established farms and businesses, and became almost indistinguishable from the Hausa among whom they lived. These town Fulani became extremely enthusiastic followers of Islam, many becoming teachers in Koranic schools. They were increasingly angered at the disregard for Islamic law and religion among the Hausa and at the hostility and persecution that some rulers showed for Muslims. Finally, one man decided to do something about the situation. This man was Shehu

Usman dan Fodio, who was then a *malami*, a teacher, who tutored the sons of the King of Gobir, the Hausa state north of Katsina. Disgusted by the corruption around him, he left the court to become an itinerant preacher, calling the people back to Islam. His success among the people soon threatened the King. It became evident that, if unchecked, this popular movement could upset the government. Shehu Usman dan Fodio fell into disfavor with the ruler, but, undaunted, he spread his preaching to the Hausa states around Gobir. The religious revival grew into holy war— a jihad—and the King of Gobir was overthrown. In each Hausa state, the Hausa ruling family was ousted by Fulani Muslims. The jihads extended south, until the rain forest and the tsetse fly checked the Muslim conquest of Nigeria.

The residents of Katsina had been warned several years previously that war was imminent. The King had decided to open a house that had been covered with red leather for hundreds of years. The elders of his council warned him that opening the house would bring war to the city. He insisted, and, when the leather was removed, thousands of white egrets flew out. Within a few years, religious revolt reached Katsina, and the Hausa King was forced to take refuge in Maradi, sixty miles north.

The presence of egrets in this legend is interesting. The white cattle egrets are slender, graceful birds, one of the pleasant sights of Katsina as they step gracefully among the feet of cattle, eating insects the herds kick up. Upon closer inspection, however, they are seen as greedy, bloodthirsty, and bellicose. In a single day in captivity, one lovely egret has been observed to eat three large toads, two mice, one beautiful fire finch, and spend the rest of the afternoon in a gruesome tug of war, trying to wrest a frog from the beak of another egret.

Whether the jihad was mounted from motives as pure as

the appearance of the egret suggests or as base as his actual character is, it is impossible to say. Muslim law forbids re-

Egrets Fighting

bellion against a King unless his evil can be proved. Shehu Usman dan Fodio wrote a long document listing the sins of the King of Gobir. He sent men to preach Islam in all of the Hausa states. Umaru Dallaje came to Katsina. The fever of the jihad was caught by Fulani across the land— a religious fervor that conveniently served to put them in power.

Like all civil wars, including Nigeria's recent tragic conflict, this one was not settled for many years. The exiled kings and their followers were referred to by the new Fulani rulers as *Habe*, a Fulani word meaning foreigners. These Habe exiles continued attempts to regain their thrones. Even as late as the end of the nineteenth century, *Habe* (Hausa) forces were plotting to ambush the Emir of Ka-

tsina as he carried his annual tribute to Sokoto. The Emir
heard of it and stayed home.

The Fulani lineage of emirs had hardly been settled for
a generation before British rule came to Katsina. Sir Fred-
erick Lugard led his troops here in 1903, formally claiming
Katsina as part of the British colony. The Emir, probably
realizing that struggle against superior forces and weaponry
was useless, welcomed him, despite the opinions of many of
his advisors.

The British governed here through indirect rule, leaving
the existing power structure intact, so long as it was efficient
and honest. The resident officer kept things in line with
British policy. Ideally, the system was supposed to benefit
both Britain and the people governed, and, in fact, it did
manage to cause less damage than colonial policy in other
parts of Africa; there was no overwhelming turmoil in
Katsina when independence was declared, because the local
rulers simply retained the positions they had occupied before and during colonial rule. Because of this, northerners
had a sound, if feudal, political base, and were able to assume a major role in the national government, a role that
was disproportionate to their number, general level of
Western-style education, and economic importance.

British rule came during a period when Katsina was somewhat out of the limelight. At the end of the fifteenth century, when the Songhai Empire fell to the Moorish invasions, Katsina had inherited the reputation for scholarship
that had once belonged to Timbuctu and Gao, because the
great Muslim scholars came to live and teach in Katsina.
Trade and the arts flourished. Nevertheless, by the beginning of the twentieth century, Katsina was paying tribute
to the Sardauna of Sokoto, who was the religious, and
therefore political, head of all Nigerian Muslims.

It was not until 1921 that the British paid any attention

to scholarship in Katsina. In that year, they established the teachers' training college. Although it was only a secondary school, it was the most ambitious in the north and the first to combine Western learning with traditional studies. It was the alma mater of the first great political leaders from the north, Sir Abubakar Tafawa Balewa, the former Prime Minister, and Sir Ahmadu Bello, the former Premier of the Northern Region and Sardauna of Sokoto.

The events leading to the civil war in Nigeria had their sources before and since independence in 1961. It would be difficult for anyone to presume to judge which side was right in this conflict. The issues became far too clouded and complicated to admit of any clear analysis or simple solution.

Katsina played no specific, individual part in the build-up to the war. As with the other cities of the north, the riots preceding the second coup in 1966 drove Ibo from Katsina. As in other cities of the federation, young men eagerly enlisted in the Nigerian Army in the recruitment campaigns after the war started in mid-1967. These young men trained enthusiastically—marching through the streets of Katsina, singing and dreaming of the adventure of war. In the years in which the war dragged on, however, it became less of an adventure and more of a burden. Although most people in Katsina believed in the necessity of a whole, federated Nigeria and believed that they are fighting a war not against the Ibo but against a rebellion, they wanted the war to end—and are now relieved that it is over.

4

Islam

NOTHING HAS DONE MORE to shape Katsina's past or present than Islam. It is more than a religion. As A. H. Kirk-Greene has written, "Islam started as a religion, became a state, and finally a culture." Practically every aspect of life in Katsina is influenced by Muslim law.

The basic tenet of Islam is "There is no god but Allah, and Muhammad is His prophet." The will of Allah is revealed by the prophet Muhammad in the Koran. Basically, a good Muslim has five duties: to have utter belief in Allah and Muhammad as His prophet, to say his prayers daily, to give alms, to fast during Ramadan, and to make the pilgrimage to Mecca at least once if he can afford it. Islam's simplicity allows for a strong adherence to, and an easy acceptance of, its tenets; it is easily spread.

Five daily prayers are required: at dawn, at about two o'clock, at around four o'clock, at dusk, and soon after dusk. The prescribed times for these prayers indicate the pattern of general daily activity in most Muslim countries. It is hot in Katsina; the work day begins soon after dawn, when it is still cool, and continues until about two o'clock. From two o'clock until the sun has moved well to the west —about four or five o'clock—it is usually too hot to do anything except rest. By late afternoon, activity starts up again: Shops open; vendors set up their stands for the night market; food sellers circulate among the people who are beginning to fill the streets.

On Friday, schools and offices close early so that everyone can go to the mosque near the Emir's palace. Although it is large, it cannot hold the tremendous influx of the faithful. (Since Friday is also market day in Katsina, the numbers often include hundreds who have come into town from villages miles away.) The field in front of the palace is filled with a mass of people, each engaged in prayer.

At these times, the prayer is usually led by the Imam. The Imam is not so much priest as teacher and authority. It is he who determines the exact dates of annual festivals, which, as part of the Muslim calendar, depend on the phases of the moon.

There are three main holidays in the Muslim year: Eid-el-Maulud, the Prophet's birthday; Eid-el-Fitri, the end of the Ramadan fast; and Eid-el-Kabir, celebrating Abraham's offer to sacrifice his son to God. Eid-el-Kabir indicates the acceptance, in Muslim law and lore, of the prophets of the religions that preceded it. For this festival, it is customary to kill a ram and share it with the poor and anyone who comes to visit during the day.

The Ramadan fast, called *azumi* in Hausa, is required by Muslim law. It begins at the sighting of the new moon of the ninth month of the Muslim calendar—in early or mid-December—and ends when the new moon of the next month is sighted.

There are special greetings exchanged during Ramadan: *"Barka da azumi"* ("Greetings on hunger") and *"Barka da shan ruwa"* ("Greetings on drinking water"), the latter said at dusk, when the people who are fasting are allowed to drink water but are not yet allowed to eat. Special prayers are also required. Fasting is observed by practically everyone, especially in an almost totally Muslim town such as Katsina. Unless one is obviously a foreigner, anyone seen eating or drinking is immediately questioned and censured. Social sanctions force even indifferent Muslims to observe the fast. Forced into fasting by social pressure, they say the prayers too. Later they can lapse again. For those for whom religion is unimportant, Ramadan is something like Christmas for indifferent Christians.

But few Hausa, especially in Katsina, are really indifferent to their religion. It is bred too deeply into them. From the time they are six or seven, children must attend several years of Koranic school, where they learn the Koran, to read and write Arabic, and are generally initiated into the knowledge of Islamic law.

Their dietary laws are similar to those of orthodox Judaism: They forbid the eating of pork and the use of alcohol or tobacco. Many Muslims circumvent the nonsmoking rule but are very conscientious about the others. Animals slaughtered for food must be killed in the prescribed manner, and the appropriate prayers must be said.

Conduct of both men and women should be modest and proper. The conduct of women is especially prescribed, and women after the age of puberty are usually kept from public view. Married women, if forced by necessity to appear in public, usually cover their heads, and sometimes their

faces, with a large shawl. Women are expected to pray and
fast, the same as men, but do not appear in public at the
mosque. Women are generally considered less pure than
men. Impurity caused by menstruation and bleeding after
childbirth cannot be cleansed by the ritual ablutions, and
women are excused from prayers at those times.

The pilgrimage to Mecca, required of those who can
afford it, is usually made during the three days of Eid-el-
Kabir, in late February or early March. Pilgrims' agents are
appointed to make the necessary elaborate arrangements. In
1969, over sixteen thousand Nigerian Muslims made the *haj*.

Women are allowed, and actually required, to make the
haj. Those who do may use the title *alhajiya*, the feminine
equivalent of *alhaji*. If a woman is pregnant while she does
the *haj*, the child born of that pregnancy may have Alhaji
as one of his given names. He is still required to make the
pilgrimage during his lifetime, however.

Most Hausa names are names of prophets, and the Muslim
list includes most of those mentioned in the Bible. Beginning with Adamu (Adam), one can continue through
familiar-sounding names—Isiaka (Isaac), Ibrahim (Abraham), Iliya (Elija)—all the way to Yusufu (Joseph) and
Isu (Jesus). Jesus is accepted as a prophet by Islam, although
most of the dogma concerning Christ is not. It seems that
half the males in Katsina have names whose base is some
form of the name Muhammad. Muhammadu, Mohmoh,
Ahmadi, Ahmed, Ahmadu, Mama, and Mamman are all
variations of the Prophet's name.

Although in its prescribed form, Islam does not contain
any sort of mysticism, its followers do not seem to be able
to rid themselves of a desire for miracles and the belief that
they occur. One can find in Katsina the tombs of several
saints, holy men about whom somewhat fantastic legends
have sprung up. For instance, the legend of Dan Marina:

Saint's Tomb near the Gobirau Mosque

His name means son of (*dan*) the dyer (*marina*). According to legend, his mother died during childbirth, and she was buried before he was actually born. He emerged while she was in the grave. Some days later, the owner of the dye pits noticed that the indigo in his pits was being disturbed every night. Someone was coming and stirring it, dropping in bits of dirt and stones from the ground around it. He sat up one night to catch the vandal. To his amazement it was a tiny child who crept up to the dye pits, played in them, and then crept away. The dyer followed the baby, and soon found himself in the graveyard, where the child was settling down to sleep in the grave of his mother. The dyer took the child and raised him with his family. He grew to be a very learned *malami* and a poet in the Emir's court.

Another Islamic scholar is buried in a small, whitewashed one-room house not far from the Gobirau mosque tower. It is a well-kept building, shaded by large tamarind trees. There is usually an old man, a *malami*, watching over the house, sweeping the compound, or sitting and meditating. Inside the room is the grave, a benchlike structure set against one wall. The top is covered by very fine white sand. People, especially women who are praying for fertility or good fortune, come to the house and take away small handfuls of it. Many believe that the sand, extremely light and smooth in contrast to the reddish-brown sand and clay dust of the countryside, appears spontaneously by some kind of minor miracle and, thus, will bring about others. But the *malami* who takes care of the grave knows that he carries in the sand from a dry river bed outside of town.

Although *malamai* can rationally explain away phenomena such as this, which common people believe to be miraculous, they, themselves, are superstitious. Many Koranic schoolteachers earn extra money by making charms—writing appropriate passages of the Koran on sheets of paper, which are folded up and wrapped in a leather pouch. Sometimes a passage is written on the wooden writing tablet, then washed off, the ink carefully saved to make a medicinal drink. Even a basically nonmystical religion such as Islam cannot seem to pull people away from belief in the supernatural.

Although people make special prayers for fertility, rain, or good fortune, and although they use amulets and charms to protect strength, the most striking feature of a Muslim in Katsina is his resignation to Allah's will. True, it can too easily be used as an excuse for mismanagement or carelessness, but only rarely can an observer find anyone who does not believe in the inevitable and irrefutable will of their god. Even among the backsliders and people who are generally indifferent to their religion, the basic belief is there, not to be erased.

When the sky turned light grey, Abdu woke up. Goats were already chewing at the fence of guinea-corn stalks around the compound, and chickens were scratching in the dust of the courtyard. Pulling his blanket around him, against the chill of the morning, Abdu stood up. Across the compound, his uncle's wives were already up, and the children were scampering around, bringing kindling for the kitchen fires and pots of water from the public tap they shared with the other compounds on the street.

Abdu called Sahia, the youngest daughter of his uncle, and she walked over to him, the clay water pot balanced neatly on her small head. She poured some water into a clay pitcher by the door of his room. Then, giggling, she ran back to the women's rooms, kicking at the chickens on her way, the heavy clay pot still balanced on her head.

He rubbed the sleep from his eyes, and pulled on the shorts and shirt he wore nearly every day. The sky was getting lighter. Soon the sun would come over the horizon.

Picking up the clay pitcher of water and the reed mat rolled up beside it, he walked out into the courtyard. It was still cold, although he knew that, by the time the sun had barely risen, it would be hot. But it was getting late. He could not waste time thinking about the weather.

He sat down on his mat and began the ritual ablutions. He washed his hands and his mouth, inhaled some water into his nostrils, then washed his face. He washed his lower arms and splashed some water onto his hair and ears. Then he washed his feet and began the dawn prayers.

He stood up, sat down, prostrated himself according to the formula, softly murmuring the Arabic words of the prayers as he went through the prescribed motions. Dimly he heard Aliyu's voice call him and then stop, as his cousin saw that he was saying his prayers and could not answer. When he had finished, he rolled up the mat, and put it and the clay pitcher away in his room. Then, he and Aliyu left the compound and walked toward the main road and the shop where they both worked.

On their way, they passed a Koranic school; about fifteen small boys were sitting on the ground under a tree, most of them reciting a verse from the Koran as loudly as they could, while the *malami* walked among them, listening to each one and soundly rapping the ones who were trying to fool him by only making sounds.

Aliyu and Abdu greeted the *malami*, crouching down respectfully as they raised their right fists. Aliyu stopped a few minutes to exchange greetings with the older boys who were sitting at the outside of the circle, carefully copying passages of the Koran onto long tablets of white wood. Aliyu had only left the Koranic school last year, when his father had decided it was time for him to start working. He had gone to this very *malami* to learn the Koran and Arabic writing. Abdu had attended a different school, in the village a few miles from Katsina where he had lived before coming to the city to work and to live in his uncle's house.

Alhaji Garba, the owner of the shop, had not yet come when Abdu and Aliyu arrived. They took their wicker brooms from a corner and began to sweep the verandah and the area in front of the shop, raising great clouds of dust, making the old beggar who sat beside the doorway complain loudly. They paid no attention, but bent down and swept harder. Alhaji Garba supported the beggar, giving him sixpence every day and letting him sit and beg in front of the shop, but the boys did not like him. They knew they were required to give some of their tiny earnings to the poor, but they preferred to give it to the blind men who sang along the main road, rather than to this bad-tempered old man who did nothing but mumble blessings or curses, depending on what the passers-by gave him.

The sun was getting higher. Alhaji Garba would come soon. He seldom came before eight o'clock, never later than nine. Salisu came down the street with his big head tray of buns and his enormous teapot. The boys called him over, and they both bought a bun and a cup of tea. Salisu sat with them, waiting for his cups and listening to the Indian music pouring out of Alhaji Labo's shop next door. Alhaji Labo had a transistor radio he played nearly every day.

Almost all the shopkeepers in Katsina were Alhajis. They all were rich enough to afford the trip to Mecca. Abdu chewed his bun and wondered what such a long journey would be like. He never really expected to make it, unless he got rich as Alhaji Garba had. He had heard that his employer was planning to make another pilgrimage this year, which meant that the shop would be closed for several weeks before and after the big Eid-el-Kabir holiday. But it also meant that he would not be getting paid for several weeks. He probably would not be able to buy new clothes for Sallah, unless Alhaji Garba gave them their Sallah dashes, or tips, before he left and, perhaps, even part of their salaries while he was gone, for watching the store during the day.

But he was coming now. Abdu handed the enamel cup back to Salisu and stood up in order to bring out the merchandise when Alhaji Garba unlocked the doors of the little shop.

There was little work that morning—just running here and there with messages or carrying boxes of cans and bottles to customers' cars. The American woman with the little girl came, the one with the very long hair; the doctor from the hospital came to buy a box of tea; and two Yoruba girls bought sweets. They were not Muslims and did not behave modestly, but they were very pretty and fun to joke with.

Abdu spent much of the morning sitting in his favorite spot, leaning against the white, metal Coca-Cola cooler on the verandah, thinking about Sallah. This would be big Sallah, Eid-el-Kabir, when everyone who could killed a ram. This killing of the ram, *laiya*, a religious ritual, meant good eating for the night.

A Sacrificial Ram

It would be the end of the month the English called— what was that funny sounding name? February? He liked big Sallah better than little Sallah, Eid-el-Fitri, mostly because for a month before Eid-el-Fitri was the fast of Ramadan. Everyone had to fast during the month of Ramadan, except for little ones such as Sahia and Aliyu's little brother Rabe, and maybe his uncle's newest wife, who was pregnant and sick all the time—and women at the bleeding time of month. The fast might hurt them or their unborn children, so they were excused. But as soon as Rabe was older and had started Koranic school, he would have to fast also and would not be able to go around eating peanuts all day long.

Not that anyone starved during Ramadan, of course. As soon as the sun went down, everyone could eat as much as he wanted. The wives of Abdu's uncle cooked special things all the time, and eating at night was the same as a big party. The bad part was that, if he did not wake up before dawn to eat breakfast, he would not have anything to eat or drink all day long. It was no good trying to sneak something, because someone might see him. Then he would be in trouble. If the Islamic judges decided it was unintentional, like waking up and taking a drink of water in the afternoon before remembering that it was the fasting time, then he would have to add an extra day of fasting after everyone else had finished. If they decided that the eating or drinking was intentional, then he could be fined, and he might have to feed as many as sixty poor people. By the time he did that, Abdu would be poor enough to go around asking for alms himself. Besides, it would seem strange to eat or drink during the fast—it would seem a real sin, even worse than the drinking of alcohol.

Sometimes, if he sat still enough in his little corner of the verandah, Alhaji Garba did not notice him and did not think of something for him to do. He would not notice him now, because he was talking to a customer—talking about Sallah and going on the *haj*, the pilgrimage to Mecca. Abdu shifted slightly in his little niche, trying to hear better.

The big customer, Alhaji something or other, was saying that the federal government in Lagos had issued the official date for Eid-el-Kabir. He worked in the Education Office, and a notice had been sent round, giving the dates the schools should be closed. But the date was wrong. It was a day early, according to the Imam in Katsina. And when it came to religious matters, the customer, for one, was more inclined to trust the religious leader of Katsina than somebody from Lagos.

Alhaji Garba was somewhat conciliatory. They would probably send around another circular in a few days. After all, there were always so many clouds in Lagos, it was a wonder anyone could see the new moon and, thus, tell accurately the beginning of the Muslim months. He had heard that the Imam in Lagos had once had to ask for an air-force jet to take him above the clouds so that he could see the moon.

The two men laughed, and Abdu tried to muffle his own giggles. He had never seen a real airplane, but the idea of an Imam's flying up into the sky with his turban and white beard was comical.

The mention of airplanes had turned the talk to the coming pilgrimage. Alhaji Garba did not like the pilgrims' agent, who was arranging the flight and lodgings, the special passports, and all the other details, including collecting fifty pounds from each pilgrim. He was going to check at the bank to be sure everything was being done properly. This was the third time he was making the *haj*, and he knew how things should be run.

Not that it was an easy job, of course, especially when more and more men were taking their wives, so they could become *alhajiyas*. Handling a pack of giggling women—now, that presented problems.

Alhaji Garba called Abdu to carry a box of canned milk and sugar to the customer's house. The box was not heavy; he hardly felt it on his head as he picked his way through the narrow passageway that led from the street to the customer's entrance hut. He amused himself by throwing small chunks of dried mud at goats, while he called, *"Salaam alaikum"* ("Peace be with you") to announce his presence. Finally, when no one came to the doorway answering, *"Alaika salamu,"* he called a little boy who was playing with a paper windmill, and asked him to go in and ask someone to come to collect the box. Better to risk Alhaji Garba getting angry at him for taking so much time than to risk entering a house with women in it, unannounced and unexpected. Soon a very old woman came and took the box from him, and he went back to the shop.

5

The Emir
of Katsina

To see the Emir of Katsina, Sir Alhaji Usman Nagogo, both as he is today and in the context of tradition, one has only to watch one of the two annual festivals of Sallah. Sallah is celebrated on the two big Muslim holidays, Eid-el-Fitri and Eid-el-Kabir, in December and February.

The day before Sallah, the horse of each district head in the Emirate is brought into town. Although the man himself will usually come to Katsina by car, the horse is led through the town with as much pomp as if the man were riding it. Early in the morning, mournful piping is heard coming from Kofar Sauri; then, the deep-pitched drumming. Finally, the procession comes into view—ten or more

The Riderless Horse of Sarkin Sullibawa Heralds the Festival of Sallah

riders in gorgeous robes, surrounding a riderless horse. It is the horse of Sarkin Sullibawa, the head of the Sullibawa branch of the royal family and chief of Kaita district. He is one of the Emir's older sons.

The music is produced by recorder-like pipes, each of which has a bulb-shaped mouth tapering to the mouthpiece. It takes real force of breath to play one, and the player's cheeks puff out larger and rounder than the bulb-shaped portion of the pipe.

Early in the morning of Sallah, the Emir, accompanied by his personal entourage and all the district heads and their entourages, rides from the palace to the prayer grounds, which are near the race course and outside the town walls. There, the Imam leads them in prayers. The horsemen need not dismount to pray. The dispensation from the usual method is necessary, since there are hundreds of horses—all stallions—many of which are nervous at the unaccustomed proximity of other horses.

After the prayers, the procession moves slowly back to town, through streets lined with people dressed in new, beautiful clothes, shouting with the excitement of seeing the Emir and the procession of all the important men in the Emirate. On these holidays, even the women in purdah

Calabash Horn

are allowed out in public. The air is filled with noise of every kind: The people in the crowds shout greetings and praises for the horsemen passing by. The music of pipes, drums, flutes, and calabash horns over six feet long competes for the attention given the dancers. The dancers keep their own rhythm with anklets of seed rattles. Some carry

Dancers at Sallah

swords and carved clubs, staging mock battles among themselves or with other groups, symbolizing age-old disputes no longer actively fought, but not forgotten. Along the way, the procession passes local showmen who wish to show the Emir a juggling feat or a great feat of strength. The crowds part a little so that he can be seen; then, the procession moves on.

The district heads are resplendent in their robes, often made of heavy velvet, brocaded with gold and silver thread. The horses glitter with gold and silver ornaments on their

Horn- and Flute-Players

A Strongman in the Sallah Procession

saddles and bridles. Some people use English saddles, but many still use the locally made Hausa saddles, not unlike American saddles with a high front and back.

As each group nears the Emir's palace, they separate from the procession and take places around the enormous field in front of the palace. The sun is high in the sky, and it is hot by this time; the trees lining the field offer some shade. Each group of musicians and dancers continues its entertainment.

The crowd presses in to watch and is beaten back with green wood switches by policemen lining the edge of the field. Anyone with a camera, though, is allowed to wander as he wishes, a concession to Westernization. The police are not being unnecessarily cruel in keeping the crowd back. The horses are extremely nervous by this time—frightened by the music, the noise, the people, the other horses. Every year, there are some accidents, and a Red Cross team roams the field carrying first-aid kits.

Important spectators—ambassadors, industrialists, state governors, the provincial secretary, the two doctors from the hospital, the principals of the three secondary schools —are afforded the safe vantage point of a balcony over the main gate to the palace. In the best of colonial traditions, they are protected from the horses, the dust, the pressing crowds. They are also kept out of the way. Nothing could be more embarrassing to the local government than to have a camel step on the foot of a visiting ambassador as he is taking a picture. The less important people of the town— schoolteachers, the chief nursing staff, the civil servants— sit in a special section under the VIP balcony.

The important people are thus seated, somewhat uncomfortably, in honor; all the others swarm around the square. All of Katsina's sixty thousand people are out today, plus thousands from the outlying towns and villages. The sun overhead is hot and bright as the hour moves closer and closer to midday. Photographers shade their eyes and consult light meters, moving from group to group amid the rhythm of drums and the high wailing of pipes.

Not all the dancers are grouped according to their districts. A group of young men dressed in tatters, their faces rubbed with indigo sediment, wanders around among the gatherings of horsemen, singing or answering taunts from the crowd. These are the bachelors and the men whose wives have left them.

An Insane Man

Individuals walk about, also. The town's insane, usually tolerated and cared for as they walk quietly about the streets lost in their own world, celebrate Sallah in their own way. One man appears wearing a rope made of thorn branches tied about his shoulders. Another, dressed in a tattered, discarded police uniform, marches behind one of the officers keeping the crowds in line, mimicking him. An old woman, dressed in a man's clothing, wanders among the horses, murmuring to herself. When they get in the way, these unfortunates are gently moved to the side. They are accepted as part of the town, part of the holiday.

Finally, horsemen come into the square carrying the green

and white flag of Katsina. The Emir's entourage has arrived. Bearing the flags are four men in white European-style uniforms, wearing red turbans. They are followed by a group of men and a few women wearing flared red tunics. These are the servants of the Emir. Their place in the procession is a remnant from the past, when the King's slaves, procured in victorious battle with other kingdoms, would thus be displayed. Behind these people walk a troop of incredibly old men, each one carrying a homemade flintlock rifle. From time to time, they fire a blast into the air, nearly bursting the eardrums of anyone within ten yards. Some of these guns, put together by local hunters, are over a hundred years old. Newer ones are made by using the central tube of the steering column of a wrecked car as the barrel. Whenever one is fired, there is a real risk that it will blow up.

A Sousa-type march is the next sound heard above the general din. The Katsina police band approaches, with drums and bugles. In the center is the big bass drum, carried by a corporal whose stomach is ample enough to sup-

The Police Band's Bass Drum

port the weight. He wears a cloak of leopard skin over his white uniform, which sports shiny brass buttons.

Behind the band is the entourage of the Magagin Garin Katsina, Alhaji Kabir Usman, Mayor of Katsina and one of the Emir's sons. He is considered most likely to become the next emir.

Finally the Emir's personal entourage comes into view. First is a camel led by a veiled Tuareg who bears a leather shield. Following this is the small bagpipe band, sounding

Magagin Garin Katsina at Sallah

and looking even more out of place on this African field than did the drum and bugle corps, considering the kilts of the Nigerian players and the Highland air they are playing. The timbre of the music, however, is much akin to the sound of the recorder-like pipes that have been wailing throughout the procession. It is not so difficult to see what attracted the Emir to them when he first visited England.

The Emir's armed guard is dressed in the manner of ancient soldiers. Vests of chain armor are visible under the swirling blue robes, and faces peer out from dark indigo turbans wrapped around the head and under the chin. They carry long spears. The personal bodyguard of the Emir is dressed in European-style uniforms—bright red coats and

The Emir's Personal Guardsmen

Bagpipe Band

white turbans. These are usually sons and grandsons of the Emir, and they all ride white horses whose manes have been plaited with red ribbons. Four of the youngest grandsons ride before the bodyguard.

Grandsons of the Emir

Finally the Emir comes, riding a splendid white horse, wearing white robes and a white turban. In his right hand, he carries a short sword of brightly polished silver. This is the sword of Katsina, dating from the thirteenth century. It is supposed to be the sword with which Korau killed Sanau at Durbi in 1260. Beside the Emir walks a servant, holding an enormous gold and red silk umbrella over the ruler's head, shading him from the glaring sun. Behind them walk three camels and their riders, who carry enormous drums. These are the ancient war drums of Katsina. Bringing up the rear of the procession is another regiment of the Emir's guard, who wear traditional robes and flat brass

The Emir of Katsina

headpieces. On closer inspection, these headpieces prove
to be brass plates with plumes stuck through the middle.

Many of the costumes and uniforms used in the Sallah
procession are traditional, dating back hundreds of years.

One of the Emir's Grandsons

Ancient War Drums of Katsina

The Emir of Katsina

The Emir's Armed Guard

Unfortunately, the traditions were broken and changed during the years of British colonial rule, and, only now, are they being reinstated. Thus, the necessity for improvisation—brass plates to imitate ancient headgear.

At the head of the field, a few yards from the palace gates, the Emir turns and faces the delegations from the districts of his Emirate.

Now the *durbar* begins. Group by group, the men of each district ride up to salute the Emir. They ride toward him at a full gallop, reining in at the last moment, so hard that the horses are pulled up on their hind legs. The men's right hands are raised in the clenched-fist greeting of the Hausa. The Emir answers them, raising his right hand, in which he holds the sword of Katsina.

The Emir's bodyguard sit on their white horses in a semicircle behind him. The riders are mostly young men—one is only fourteen. They are as nervous about their horses as the horses are about the people pressing around them and the other horses racing toward them. Little attention is paid to the task of actually guarding the Emir; they are too busy controlling their mounts.

The delegations from the districts rush up in a fury. The crowd pushes and shoves to see the Emir. Only the Emir is calm in the midst of the storm, smiling at his people. Behind the smile, what is he thinking? Once again, his power is asserted and recognized; once again, he affirms himself as ruler of these people. These thoughts undoubtedly pass through his mind. But, some of the time, he is looking over the horses being ridden up to him, noting which ones he would like to add to his stable. After Sallah, there is always a new horse or two on the polo field or at the races. The Emir is president of both the Nigerian Polo Association and the Northern States Turf Club.

After the final district has saluted him, the Emir's armed

guard, in their coats of mail and enormous blue turbans, ride up for the last salute. Then the Emir speaks to the assembled crowd, telling them what to expect in the coming year, praising them for their loyalty, and urging them to continue as good Muslims and as good men of Katsina.

The Emir, mounted on his magnificent white stallion, carries a sword that is at least seven hundred years old. He stands there as his father, as all the emirs of his lineage have stood, as the kings of the Habe lineage have stood, receiving the feudal homage of his people. But above him stretch the telephone and electric wires of twentieth-century Katsina, and he delivers his speech not by shouting above the noise of the crowd but by speaking softly into a microphone that sends his voice through the streets of Katsina. He holds the sword of state, but his power is diminished, and will diminish still further in the years to come, for Katsina is no longer a law unto itself but is a part of a nation—a nation which is pushing itself into the arena of industrial world powers.

The Emir is not a figurehead, not by any stretch of the imagination. If one day he decided to order his men to march against their old enemy, the Kano Emirate, he would find, without trouble, regiments that would follow his orders. They would have no hope of defeating Kano. But many men would march to war on the orders of their Emir, not only the old men with flintlock rifles who dream of the years when they marched to real wars on the orders of this Emir's father but also younger men whose lives are firmly entrenched in this modern world.

One of the reasons that the Emir of Katsina retains his power is that he does not choose to show it in useless exercises such as declaring a senseless war. He is, instead, the head of the local government, working within the framework of the national government.

After seeing him at the center of the Sallah procession, one is surprised, at a less formal meeting, to see that the Emir is a rather short, slender, but strongly built man. His extremely expressive eyes, which convey both strength and good humor, are his most striking feature. Were it not for the Emir's clothes, which are somewhat finer than most other men's, and his walk, which speaks of total confidence in himself, a stranger might not realize, at first glance, that he is indeed the Emir. Of course, he does not walk about the streets casually, so there is usually little danger of his being snubbed by some ignorant stranger.

He is nearly seventy years old and still extremely fit. He plays polo almost every week, although he has retired from tournament competition. He attends the races in Katsina and tours throughout his Emirate several times a year.

The Emir lives within a labyrinth of a palace that holds, in addition to his personal residence, meeting rooms for district heads and the Local Authority Council. When going

The Local Authority Council Building

One of the Emir's Advisers Standing Before the Palace

through the palace gates, one first sees a tree-lined drive, with a parking lot on one side. Directly at the head of the drive is the building housing the office of the Emir's secretary, Alhaji Sule. To the left is the entrance to the Emir's residence.

Often, if he is expecting someone, he will be sitting on a lawn chair on the verandah. The servants of the palace are around him, perhaps showing him the first produce of the royal farms, perhaps presenting him with problems and petitions. He always seems to listen to these people with understanding and compassion.

To enter the residence, one goes through a mud-brick entrance room, much the same as that of any other Hausa dwelling—except that this has a high, valuted ceiling and walls that are several feet thick. The first room one enters is a large reception hall. Thick blue carpets cover the floor, and the walls are lined with armchairs. This is where most of the Emir's formal audiences are held. Beyond this room is the trophy room, another large room filled with arm chairs and covered with beautiful carpets. Over the carpets, here and there, are the skins of leopards or large antelopes the Emir or his father has shot. The end of the room is filled with a large glass case where gleaming silver trophies are displayed. Most of them are for racing, for the Emir and his father were ardent horsemen, and the palace has a stable full of extremely fine horses. Several are polo cups: the Georgian cup, the highest prized cup in Nigeria; an international trophy from a tournament in England; and other, lesser cups from Nigeria. A picture on the wall shows one of the first polo teams in Katsina—the Emir, two of his brothers, and the British resident officer. The picture, taken in the 1930's, shows a very young version of the man standing beside us. Not all the trophies are for sports. The Emir takes a silver cigarette case from a shelf in the glass case. This was presented to him when he visited the Katsina regiment in Burma during World War II.

From the trophy room, one follows a short passageway to the Emir's private garden and guest house. There is a small fountain in the corner—a luxury that speaks of more than money in this arid part of the world. The gravel walks meander among rose bushes, jasmine, hibiscus, and the air is heavy with their sweet perfume. There is a gravel area in front of the verandah of the guest house. This is where the Emir holds his annual cocktail party during the Katsina tournament.

Through another doorway is the barnyard. There, the day before Sallah, one can find twenty white horses being curried and brushed, their manes plaited in red ribbons, their white coats shining in the bright sunlight. These stables hold only some of the Emir's horses. Others are kept at his farm, outside the town walls. In the palace barnyard, he also keeps other livestock—dairy and beef cattle; prize sheep; and a young, spirited bull, imported from England to improve local stock, who breaks loose from his keepers whenever he can, to greet visitors enthusiastically.

Beyond the barnyard is another of the Emir's sitting rooms. Few visitors penetrate further into the labyrinth than this. One gets the impression that it extends far, far back—each room opening onto another, each doorway leading to yet another garden. Every successive Emir has enlarged the palace, according to his personal whims. Looking at the high ceilings, the thick walls, it is not hard to imagine scenes from the *Arabian Nights*. Indeed, when he strolls through his palace, his feet shod in embroidered slippers, wearing under his robes a wide-sleeved jacket embroidered in silver, the Emir does resemble a sheik in one of those tales. One look at the glint of laughter in his eyes at these moments, and one is sure that he, too, sees the resemblance, and thoroughly enjoys it.

The *Arabian Nights* image is somewhat deceptive, however, for the Emir is not extravagant and does not collect exorbitant taxes to use for his own pleasure. He is, indeed, quite frugal, compared to other emirs and the politicians of the old civilian government. He rides in a shiny red Oldsmobile, glittering with chrome trim, seemingly yards longer than it is, which presents a sharp contrast with the donkeys and bicycles—the traditional means of transport.

The car is over eight years old, so lovingly cared for that it retains the original paint finish, still shiny and unmarked.

It would be impossible to do away with the traditional rulers in Nigeria abruptly, even if the government wanted to do so. They are firmly entrenched. But, bit by bit, the national government is cutting down their actual power.

Under the former system, in which Nigeria was divided into four regions, the Northern Region, the Western Region, the Midwestern Region, and the Eastern Region—the Northern Region occuped nearly two-thirds of the country. Even when the region was divided into provinces, it was an enormous job for the central regional government to handle it. So the national government gladly followed the British colonial system of allowing the emirs to continue administering their own areas, so long as their administration did not contradict national policy.

With the creation of states in 1967, however, the administrative burden was spread out, and the power of the emirs was reduced. Even the emirates themselves were cut down in size. Two towns, about one hundred miles from Katsina, formerly in the Emirate, were set up as an independent administrative unit.

Perhaps the greatest advantage in retaining the emirs is that they help to preserve the sense of grace, of politesse, of contact with the pleasant old ways. An Emir maintains a closeness with the people; although royal, he is one of them. A governor cannot be that close. People write letters to newspapers to complain of this or that governmental policy; they do not complain about the Emir—simply because he is the Emir.

He also is closely connected with the religion of the region. The holidays Eid-el-Fitri and Eid-el-Kabir might be meant to be devoted to prayer and religious thoughts, but a Sallah without the pageantry of the *durbar* (the headlong gallop of district representatives to greet the Emir) would be an empty holiday. It is interesting to see how the national government has been brought into the traditional sphere in these Sallah celebrations. Sallah is a two-day celebration: the first day is devoted to the Emir, to tradition; on the second day, all the delegations from the districts, together with the Emir and his entourage, ride out to the provincial secretary's lodge, some two miles out of town, in the government residential area. There, the provincial secretary, the main representative of the national government, receives homage from the procession. There is, however, no breath-taking *durbar* but only a more sedate march around the semicircular driveway of the lodge. The provincial secretary delivers his speech to the people and then serves roast ram and soft drinks. The "people" gathered on his lawn, of course, are not the crowds who packed the square in front of the palace but the important people of the town, who come by invitation and sit comfortably on folding chairs. Crowds, however, gather outside on the road, and the dancers and mock fighters, the musicians and jugglers go through their routines.

The provincial secretary and the Emir, while always friendly in public are always somewhat at odds in official policy. One gets the impression that the provincial secretary, whose tenure in office is not long, may win most of the time but that his victories never really affect the Emir excessively. One example involved the enrollment of several of the Emir's daughters in Katsina Women's Teachers' College. The provincial secretary used this as an example to other people of the town; he tried to encourage the idea of Western education for women. He even enrolled his own wife as a student there. After a year or two, however, the Emir decided to have his daughters withdrawn, because they were passing the usual marriage age. There ensued an argument the details of which one can only guess. The Emir's daughters returned to class, which represented a small victory for the provincial secretary, but the Emir had many daughters—over twenty of them—and could easily afford to give a few to progress. The rest can stay properly cloistered in Hausa and Muslim tradition. Thus, both he and the provincial secretary won.

Years ago, the Emir of Katsina encouraged one of his sons, Hassan, to take a commission in the army. This was unprecedented for an Emir, whose sons were expected to take traditional posts in local government or to become religious teachers. Perhaps the Emir made his decision because he knew that Hassan was of a somewhat rebellious nature and might be better off in the army, where he would not be constantly restrained by traditional conventions.

At the time of the first coup, Hassan Katsina had risen to the rank of colonel, and was named governor of the Northern Region. After the second coup, he became chairman of the Northern States Interim Council, a body supervising the turnover from the old regional government to the new states. When, in 1968, the states actually came into being, Colonel Hassan Katsina was promoted to the rank of brigadier and was named Chief of Staff of the Nigerian Army. In a military government like Nigeria's, this position is very near the top. Although father and son might have had great battles when Hassan was young, they hold each other in mutual respect now.

The Emir, being a Muslim and having four wives as his religion permits, has many sons. Some, of course, are obscure—schoolteachers, clerks in offices. There is not enough room at the top for all of them. Only a few can be named district heads or groomed for succession to the emirship. The heritage of the others remains some social and genealogical prestige and the unmistakable physical and mental qualities that characterize the present royal family.

There is one man in Katsina for whom being son of the Emir is totally meaningful—one man who walks with as much confidence in his stride as the Emir. This is the Magagin Garin Katsina, Alhaji Kabir Usman, the mayor of Katsina and next in line for the emirship. Physically, he resembles his father: rather short, slender, but strong in build. The eyes are much the same: expressive, at times a bit wild, and always seeming to express a hint of laughter. He is more of the modern world than is his father. He moves with equal grace and dash at a cocktail party and in the Sallah procession. He is listened to with the same respect by both Nigerians and expatriates.

6

Sports and
Social Life

MENTION KATSINA to anyone involved in sports in Nigeria, and he will think of polo. Therein lies a paradox.

Polo, to most people, brings images of Prince Philip, of the British Colonial Army, of incomprehensible upper-class idiosyncrasies. These images are, for the most part, justified. But the paradox is twisted and retwisted.

Polo originated in Persia hundreds of years ago. It was a vastly different game then, with twenty or more players on each side—more of a battle exercise than a sport. It spread across the Arab world wherever horses were readily available. The British, in the days of the empire, picked it up. When horsemanship was an essential part of soldiering, it seemed, as no doubt it had seemed to the Persians, an excellent military sport.

When the British Empire expanded to Nigeria, polo came to the country. Anywhere the tsetse fly did not preclude keeping horses, polo teams were started for recreation. Nigerians took part as horsekeepers and field-cleaners.

The resident officer in Katsina must have felt frustrated. Katsina, out of the way and relatively unimportant, did not have enough of a British population to make up a team. In 1924, the father of the present Emir, who, himself, was an enthusiastic sportsman, when presented with the idea of polo, had prisoners clear a field, lent horses to the British players in town, and urged his sons to learn the game. In 1929, the Katsina team was in the finals of the Georgian Cup tournament, the biggest polo competition in Nigeria. It was the only team at that time that included Nigerians.

The Hausa and Fulani are natural horsemen. Most families of any wealth have at least one horse, whether entered in races, maintained for the two annual Sallah processions, or just used for riding from town to town. Children learn to ride early—every year in Sallah, boys of five or six ride proudly in the procession. Horses are easily available and much cheaper than they would be in England or the United States—within the reach of a fairly affluent Nigerian. A very good horse could cost from twenty to thirty pounds—between $50 and $75.

In Nigeria, then, polo is not necessarily the sport of rich men. In Katsina especially, the Emir has always encouraged the local authority police and other civil servants to play polo. The horses of the mounted police can be rented by the month by players who do not have their own horses. Thus, Katsina and many other towns in the north can send all-Nigerian teams to tournaments against old-guard expatriate teams—and win.

Polo-tournament week in Katsina is as big a social event as Sallah. The day before it begins, players from Kano,

Kaduna, Daura, Sokoto, and Zaria come to town. During the preceding week, their horses have been coming by truck, and these are stabled in the police compound. On a quiet Sunday afternoon, the silence is broken by a sound one seldom hears in Katsina. An airplane is flying low over the town, bringing Brigadier Hassan. His brothers have gone from the Emir's palace to greet him at the airport.

Sunday evening there is a practice game—a free-for-all in which the players ride their horses over the field, letting them get used to it and work out the kinks that have developed in their muscles during the days of travel and of stabling in strange places. It is November. The dry season has just begun, and there is still some grass on the field. In the morning, tractors pulling tanks of water will sprinkle the field to hold down the dust. After only an hour of practice riding, the dust flies up and the players can hardly see the ball.

At midafternoon of the next day, the tournament begins. The hour is three-thirty, and the sun is still glaring and hot, but, to fit in all the games for the two cups, three games must be played each day. A few enthusiasts are already sitting on the grandstand, a mud-brick and cement structure. There is one wide platform about thirty feet long and ten feet wide, now packed with folding chairs. From the back, a separate set of steps leads up to a tower-like projection. This is where the Emir sits during the tournament.

Two hundred yards away, across the width of the field, the horses are standing in the shade of a small grove of trees. On the spectators' platform is a small table where the timekeepers sit. Their job, and the jobs of the goal judges and the scorekeeper (he posts the numbers on the blackboard at the far side of the field) are given to expatriates. One can only wonder whether this is an attempt to pull the somewhat distant expatriate community into local life or a subtle way of putting foreigners in their place. In cities where polo is still mainly an expatriate game —Lagos or Kaduna, for example—these menial jobs are handled by Nigerians.

By three-fifteen, the horses are all in place. The players pace nervously, checking saddles and sticks. The Magagin Gari, captain of the main Katsina team, drives up in his pale green Citroën with four or five players. Greetings are exchanged. Here is Alhaji Lafene, a former provincial secretary, now posted to Sokoto; finding no polo team in Sokoto, he organized one himself. Here is Alhaji Yusufu Katsina, younger brother to the Magagin Gari, a schoolteacher recently posted from Katsina to Zaria, where he, too, has organized a polo team. The brigadier arrives in his army-olive Mercedes.

Far down the road a shout rises, and then comes closer. The Emir is coming, and people by the side of the road are greeting him. The bright red Oldsmobile pulls up to the steps of the grandstand. The players circle around him and greet him; then he mounts to his tower. The brigadier is not playing in the first game, and he sits with his father. The crowd that had filled the road when the Emir was coming now fills the spectators' area around the field.

It is three-thirty, and, although minutes before it did not seem that the game could possibly start on time, now the players have mounted and are crossing the field in a line with the umpires. About ten yards from the stands, they stop and lift their polo sticks in a salute to the Emir. Then, they line up for the throw-in.

Basically, polo operates according to the same principles as soccer or hockey—one team, in this case four men on horseback, tries to drive a ball through the goal posts of the opposing team. The ball is a little bigger than a tennis ball and is made of very light-weight bamboo root, painted a glossy white. The sticks used are usually made of bamboo cane, about four feet long, with cigar-shaped heads about ten inches long and an inch and one-half in diameter. The long, flat part of the head, not the narrow end, is used to hit the ball.

The rules of play are simple. Direction of play is changed after each goal, and no one is allowed to play in a way that will endanger other players or himself. There is an invisible line between the ball and the last person who hit it, and anyone who crosses that line closer than five yards to an oncoming player is penalized. This is true, even if the two players are on the same team. Prime regard is for the horses. If a man falls, the game continues; if a horse falls, time out is called.

Later in the tournament week, the governor of the state will arrive, to play in a friendly match and to present the cups. In 1967, the chief of the Nigerian Air Force came; on the final day of the tournament, spectators were alarmed at the sight of two MIG jets (recently purchased from the Soviet Union) buzzing the field.

Polo and Sallah are the two "horsey" events that bring droves of important visitors to Katsina. Equally exciting, but not such a drawing card, are the races, held three or four times a year. The race course is outside of town, about a mile up the Jibya road. Competitors come from Katsina, from Maradi in the Niger Republic, and from all over the Emirate. There is no starting gate, and a great deal of time is spent lining the horses up and getting them to start together. Once, there were ten false starts before the race got under way.

The jockeys are an ill-assorted group, some having the classic jockey build, others standing over six feet tall. Their gear ranges from silk shirts and riding boots to singlets and bare feet. But the horses could hold their own on any race track in the world. A favorite is the Emir's big white stallion Sultan, who consistently wins or places in the races here and in other cities.

The races offer, besides their intrinsic excitement, a testing ground for polo ponies. Prospective buyers approach the owners of horses placing fifth or sixth, because the owners of the winners would prefer running their horses in additional races.

Although gambling is disapproved of in the Koran, it is one of the more popular sins in Katsina. Numerous bets are placed—and the biggest betters are from among the brightly dressed contingent of unmarried ladies from town, who have a sizable income and are certainly free to come to the races on a Saturday afternoon.

Katsina may be a dusty, sleepy-looking town, but there is seldom a lack of entertainment. The Hausa culture instills a strong social sense and provides an efficient social organization. The community meets many social needs, including entertainment.

The social cohesion makes itself evident in various ways. For example, in the Hausa system of naming, there is no surname that lasts through generation after generation. A child is given a first name; later in life, he can decide to use his father's first name as a surname, or he can use the name of the town where he was born—thus, names such as Hassan Katsina and Lawal Kaita are not uncommon. This evidence of community spirit labels a man by his birthplace, even after he has left it.

Another evidence of social cohesion is the existence of fads. Overnight, everyone on the streets throughout the north will be wearing some particular piece of jewelry or clothing. During the early months of the civil war, someone devised a twopenny necklace of plastic thread, with a pendant of plastic thread woven into a cylinder or box. This was called Ojukwu's beard or Ojukwú's coffin. Within a week, these were on sale in every Hausa market and then were around the neck of every Hausa child.

Part of the social organization is based on the almost feudal set-up of classes and the limited social mobility. The popular acceptance of class distinctions, the absence of revolutionary sentiments that often comes when a feudal society is exposed to a foreign society based on more democratic principles, is, perhaps, a result of the willingness of the upper classes to contribute to public entertainment, as well as to public welfare.

There are "gentlemen's football games," in which respected men of the town go out on the stadium field and kick a football around. The attitude of the players runs from serious competition to outrageous clowning. The combination produces a spectacle that brings the important men of the town down to the level of the ordinary citizen. In the same way, games between improbable groups, such as the beggars and the unmarried ladies, bring the lower levels of society up to the rest of society, at least for the duration of the game.

Not all sports, of course, are meant to be comic. The local schools regularly compete with each other and with schools of other towns in soccer, field hockey, basketball, and track.

Games period at Katsina Teachers' College starts at four-thirty. The field is rough; the dried grass, cutting, with lumps of loose dirt dried hard as rocks. Yet most of the boys play with bare feet, the calluses on the soles of their feet as tough as shoe leather. The sun is low—the game does not start until the heat becomes bearable. A crowd has formed around the football field—students from Katsina Teachers' College and the Government Secondary

School, in varying degrees of proper uniform, as well as children from primary schools or from the Koranic schools, which have released students until the evening prayer call.

On the field next to that devoted to the football game, a hockey game is in progress. Field hockey is a girls' sport in most American high schools and colleges, but here it is played in as masculine and rough a way as the version on ice. The ball flies; sticks flail; shinbones are struck hard by sticks or by the ball.

On a court nearer the school buildings, a few teachers join in the less strenuous game of volleyball, a game that gives vent to a few boys' slapstick sense of humor. While fifty yards away their classmates are slashing viciously at one another's legs with hockey sticks, the volley ball team specializes in knock-kneed pirouettes.

On other courts, gamesmasters are introducing newer games—tennis and basketball. (Katsina, and most towns in the north, are able to have spacious games areas because there is little difficulty in keeping them cleared. In southern Nigeria, there is a constant struggle to keep the bush back, and after every long holiday, several days must be spent clearing the games fields.)

Basketball, since it involves less personal equipment than tennis, is growing in popularity, and there always seems to be a young American around to coach a team. Tennis is liked mainly because it is a prestige sport, but students precariously keeping their balance on the pebble-strewn courts know that they will have few chances to play when they are assigned to teach in primary schools in small bush villages.

Anyone who drives out through Kofar Sauri to the government residential area during games period will probably find the sides of the road lined with young men in red singlets and green track shorts. These are boys from the

Government Secondary School, practicing cross-country running. Only a few seem serious about it, jogging steadily along. Most of them, practicing because of coercion rather than from choice, are walking, poking at anthills with sticks, kicking stones, or trying to flag down passing cars to hitch a ride.

Organized school sports are not the only recreation open to young people in Katsina. Numerous clubs play each other in football, and any stretch of open ground will probably have a few boys kicking a ball around or knocking at stones with improvised hockey sticks. Smaller children have simpler games—rolling a wire hoop with a stick or driving an imaginary car, devised of two small wire wheels, with the axle attached to a long, straight wire that ends in a steering wheel. If this is too complicated or expensive, children devise pinwheels of colored paper and sticks. During a certain season—after the harvest, when guinea-corn stalks stripped of their grain are drying in the fields—a multitude of toy trucks and airplanes appear. Cleverly and painstakingly constructed from the pithy center of the corn stalks, the centers are laid in rows and pinned together with slivers of the outer peel. The designs range from simple boxlike trucks to elaborate jet airplanes, painted with colored ink, with wheels made of sun-baked clay, and fancy details such as windows supplied by bits of cigarette-wrapper cellophane.

Manufactured toys were once absent from Nigerian childhood, but several Nigerian plastic companies recently started putting out a large line of simple toys—fish, dolls, birds, cats with squeakers, racing cars, and boats—each selling for less than a shilling (fourteen cents). These are hawked from the head trays of street vendors, and nearly every child in Katsina now has at least one plastic toy as well as his hoops and sticks.

A Model Airplane Made of
Guinea-Corn Stalks

Not all entertainment is athletic; nor is it all confined
to children or daytime. In the early part of the evening, the
major attraction is the movies. It is open air, like a drive-in,
although customers walk in and sit on benches or folding
chairs. The attractions are usually Indian films, with
dubbed-in English or English subtitles and with complicated, incomprehensible plots brimming with action. The
plot is unimportant to the audience, most of whom do not
understand much English. But the action is loudly cheered,
villains booed, and love scenes greeted with shouts and
whistles of encouragement. Sometimes the fare will be
varied with grade-B epics (*Hercules Meets the Dragon
Monsters*) or ancient American films (such as the serial
adventures of Jesse James, spliced together so that every
ten minutes the hero is in dire peril—perhaps bound and
gagged beside a barrel of dynamite, the fuse of which is
burning shorter and shorter).

After the movies, especially on weekends, dances at one of the three hotels in town draw the more energetic crowds. The Hamdala and the Arewa occasionally have big-name bands from the worldlier cities of Kano or Kaduna: five or six men with guitars, amplifiers, a saxophone or trumpet, drums, which are most important, and a repertoire of West African, American, and European songs. The entertainment at these hotels, like the movies, takes place in the open air. Since it rains only during four months out of the year, and even then not more than once or twice a week, why bother with a ceiling? The tables are arranged around the dance floor, and, when the tables are filled, customers sit on folding chairs or on the ground. When the music is being played, there are few enough people sitting down.

When there are no bands in town, there are records or Tambola, a kind of lottery that gives the hotel the air of Bingo night at the Elks Club, with everyone eagerly watching his ticket and listening to the announcements of the drawing. From time to time, a social club in town, such as the Medical Social Club—comprising the nursing staff of the hospital—the police, or the hotel itself will hold a dance, sometimes adding to the attraction by staging a beauty contest.

An ordinary dance just begins. The band starts playing, then one or two people begin to dance and the floor fills— some men dance by themselves, because there is always a shortage of women at the dances. People dance, drink, talk, argue.

A dance organized by a social club, however, is different. Programs are printed; the president and the secretary of the club give speeches; an honored guest says a few words; the dances are introduced; and the people are coyly urged to dance. The judges for the beauty contest are selected from the audience: two prominent men whose judgment will not be questioned, a quiet woman whose husband's judgment will not be questioned, perhaps an expatriate woman. Men bring shy, giggling girls onto the dance floor. Numbers are pinned on their dresses, and the band begins to play. As the girls circle the dance floor, the judges cancel out the obvious losers. The president of the club might come and tell the judges that certain girls should win, because they are members of the club or because they are girlfriends of special people—advice that the judges usually accept with good grace.

A dance provides a good opportunity to observe most varieties of dress in Katsina. Women's clothes range from Western-style dresses, often made from Kampala cloth—of a tie and dye pattern, originally made with local indigo dye, which now is manufactured commercially in hundreds of shades and patterns—to variations of the traditional blouse and wrapper. The traditional dress can be richly fashioned of satin, brocade, or velvet or simple—a cotton wrapper with a matching cotton blouse or jersey. Great skill goes into tying a wrapper, which is just a yard or two of cloth with no special cut or pattern. It must be fastened so securely—with no buttons, snaps, or ties—that there is never any danger of its falling off. One of the provocative moves of the dance is to loosen the wrapper and adjust it slightly. The trick is to do this without awkwardly exposing oneself.

Women usually wear their hair plaited into several braids and covered with some sort of headdress. The Yoruba style is elaborate, usually standing a full ten inches from the top of the head. A more usual style among the Hausa in Katsina is a scarf tied around the head in the gypsy style, with the knot at the nape of the neck.

Jewelry is necessary. No woman is ever without earrings and some kind of necklace. They might be custom-made gold trinkets from the goldsmith in town, or three-penny gold-painted junk from the market. A woman does not forgo jewelry because she cannot afford something beautiful.

For men, the style of dress varies more than for women. At a dance, one or two of the more important men will be wearing European business suits and ties. Others might be wearing slacks and a shirt of some kind. Many more will wear the modern Nigerian formal dress: trousers and a loose-fitting jacket, designed to be worn without a shirt and tie. This style, called a Kano State in Katsina, is subject to as many variations as the imagination of the tailor is capable. It is usually made of fairly expensive lightweight suiting in colors and patterns from conservative solid greys and browns to ultracool stripes and plaids. The trousers may be cut straight, tapered, bell-bottomed, or in a style called VC-10 (jokingly referred to as "Keep Lagos Clean"), with the trousers fitting to just below the knee, then flaring out, with an inverted pleat along the outside of the calf. This last is pretty rich fare for Katsina and was only seen on a few very sophisticated students. The jacket of a Kano State suit can have a sport-shirt–type collar; a round, collarless neck; or a high, Mao-coat, mandarin collar. The most popular style is the round neck.

Nigerian men, particularly the Hausa, normally keep their heads covered. The most usual hat is a round cap made from cotton and is hand embroidered. Young boys on the street pass their time by making these caps. The cap is entirely covered with multicolored embroidery in geometric patterns. The same shaped cap can be bought without the embroidery—just a white cotton skullcap. Anyone connected with the Emir, either of his family or staff, is entitled to wear a red felt cap, much the same shape as the cotton ones. The embroidered cotton caps are made in

Nigeria; most of the felt ones come from Czechoslovakia.

A few years ago, a man's ethnic group and station in life could be identified by the cap he wore. But lately, perhaps in response to the heavy "one Nigeria" propaganda, styles of other tribes have become popular. One is the Kampala, which was originally Yoruba tie and dye, but is now popular all over Nigeria. Men wear shirts of it as often as women wear dresses or wrappers of it. Another popular style is the Yoruba cap, tall and cylindrical, worn with the top folded over to the side or front.

The Kano State suit is a popular compromise between European dress and traditional clothing. In Katsina, more than in the south, the traditional *riga* (see p. 26) is still worn on all occasions by most men. It has the double advantage of being rich and impressive while being cool and comfortable. Underneath the *riga*, a man might wear a typical Hausa jacket, long-sleeved or sleeveless, sleek-fitting, made of felt in dark colors—olive, brown, black—with elaborate embroidery on the sleeves and down the front. The variations in men's fashions, even in an unsophisticated town like Katsina, are much greater than the variations in women's styles.

The dance itself, the "high life," is another combination of the modern and the traditional. Its underlying rhythms and movements go far back into the West African past. Its sound and sense are of today. The basic step is simple—two steps backward with one foot, two steps backward with the other. The shuffling of feet on the cement dance floor provides the beat under the music. Over this basic step, the body and arm movements are entirely the prerogative of the dancers. Often two good dancers will act out a pantomime of provocation and pursuit, the hip and hand motions becoming explicit.

The music is local or imported from the Congo, sometimes overlaid with Western sounds. The themes are usual for popular music—love and its related emotions. remorse, joy, hope. Some are political: "Ojukwu Bye-bye," "To Keep Nigeria One Is a Task that Must Be Done," "Major General Yakubu Gowon." The political motif is usually represented by the repetition of national slogans in the midst of the music.

At one hotel in the town, modern music is not played. On a small raised platform, at one end of the narrow court-yard, sit men drumming giant half-calabashes, playing high-pitched melodies on a one-stringed violin made from a smaller calabash. This is *goge*, the violin, the music, the erotic dance that is done with it. In *goge*, the audience does not participate, but teams of dancers tour the hotels of the region.

At all the hotels, the girls who are dancing, sitting, drinking, and talking are almost all unmarried ladies from town. Muslim wives are not brought to public places, especially not to bars and dances, although a few Yoruba or Tiv girls might be there with their dates or husbands. The Hausa ladies cater to the social needs of the Hausa man, which would otherwise be unmet because of the strict purdah in which he keeps his wives. Some of the girls at these hotels may be hard-boiled prostitutes, but many simply are pro-viding company and a dance partner for the evening.

7

Rites of Passage: Important Events in Hausa Life

HAUSA FAMILY LIFE is arranged in such a way that a stranger might never penetrate it, but friends and relatives can be familiar with every detail, every child's mishap, every marital quarrel. The dwellings have already been mentioned. Heavy walls of mud brick face the street; the doorway leads into an empty reception room with a few mats rolled in a corner and perhaps a hoe. Before entering, one must call, "*Salaam alaikum*" until someone inside answers. Entering a Hausa home uninvited is forbidden.

The wives live on one side of the courtyard, each in a separate room with her children. The husband has another room, and other relatives are placed wherever there is room. Inside the room of each wife, the walls are lined with shelves of enameled pots and plates. Every Hausa woman comes to marriage with hundreds of these brightly colored vessels. Few are actually used; the rest are used to decorate the walls and display wealth.

The bed may be a thick straw mat on a mud-brick ledge or on the floor, but the family usually provides a metal bedstead, the frame kept polished and gleaming. Clothes are kept in boxes, usually metal, stored under the bed or around the walls of the room. There are few other possessions kept here, few needed. There might be a stool or two, a small bench, a box of cosmetics, a kerosene lamp.

The pattern varies little if the family is of the educated class. The layout of the house remains the same. Perhaps, the mud-brick walls will be covered with cement and whitewashed. More furniture might be added—a refrigerator, bookshelves. It is a convenient style of house, adapted to the climate, and there is little reason to change it.

The utter seclusion of women is practised only in so far as it is practical. Probably no stranger has ever seen the wives of the Emir or of the prominent men in town. They can afford to keep their women entirely out of the view of the world. But, for the poorer farmer, this is more difficult. Unless the family is very big, he needs his wife's help in the fields during the busy planting and harvesting times. And if there is no small child to send to do the marketing, she must go herself. If she makes bean cakes to sell, someone must go out and sell them. Keeping an adolescent daughter in purdah is even more difficult. The wife has come to depend on her to run errands, to sell porridge or cakes, and the girl enjoys her freedom. Yet, if the daughter is allowed to circulate in public after a certain age, she is subject to influences and temptations that may lessen her chances of making a good marriage.

Hausa children are prepared for the roles they will play in life almost from the very moment of their birth. The

A Young Girl Vending Fried Bean Cakes

circumstances surrounding birth itself are prescribed by both Hausa custom and Muslim law. Very few children are born in hospitals—hospital space and staff are too limited to care for any but the most complicated maternity cases—and most women shy away from having a child in strange, foreign surroundings.

An older woman of the family, a senior wife or elder sister, is midwife. She cuts the umbilical cord and treats the wound until it heals. The mother is washed with hot water, an infusion of herbs, and the bark of the fig or acacia tree. Custom dictates that she continue these baths twice a day for forty days after the birth, then once a day for forty more days. This varies according to the climate of the region. In the eleventh and twelfth centuries, Muslim physicians were practicing medicine very close to twentieth-century standards, and this forms the basis of much of the Muslim traditional laws and customs concerning childbirth. If the ritual baths are taken, chances of avoiding the infections, which can accompany childbirth, are good.

The mother usually goes to her parents' home for the birth of her first child, and spends forty to eighty days there. There, she is trained in the care of the newborn infant and in her own personal hygiene. She is taught by her own mother and female relatives.

About seven days after the birth, there is a naming ceremony. Among the Hausa, it is the father who selects the name of the child, male or female. During the seven days before the naming ceremony, the new mother need not assume her household duties. The baby is washed and cared for by the midwife or another female relative and brought to the mother for feeding. The household chores are undertaken by relatives or neighbors.

A Hausa child is given several names, one of which is the name of one of the prophets or companions of Muhammad. Another name might refer to circumstances surrounding the birth—the day of the week; the time of the year; the place in the family, such as that of the first son after two or more daughters, a child born after several previous children have died in infancy or after a set of twins.

For the naming ceremony a male goat, ram, or bull is slaughtered by a *malami*, who offers the prayers and utters the name of the child. Then the *malami* announces the name to the crowd of guests. Often praise singers from town will come, uninvited, and wander among the crowd, shouting extravagent praises of the newborn child and the

A *Malami*, or Koranic Teacher

entire family. The *malami* and three other guests offer prayers. At the close of the third prayer, the ceremony is over, and the guests disperse. As they leave, the father makes payments in money and in meat from the slaughtered animal. The *malami*, the praise singers, the butchers who skinned and cut up the meat, the midwife, the women who have been doing the housework, all are given a portion of meat and some money or cloth.

A barber then comes. He shaves the head of the child, removes the uvula, and makes any facial marks the father may wish. The custom of facial scarification is dying out in Nigeria, but a few children, especially in villages, are still marked. Hausa markings are usually a very fine tracery of lines. Sometimes powdered charcoal is rubbed into the wounds to make the marks dark; sometimes the lines are left alone and only a thin line of scar tissue marks the incisions. The markings are usually not disfiguring, even to Western observers. One seldom sees evidence in adults that the incisions had become infected when they were children. The incisions are very shallow, and the Muslim tradition of cleanliness helps to prevent infection.

If the child is a girl, the ears are pierced at this time. This is done by punching a threaded needle through the ear lobe, then tying the thread in a loop. The string is moved around every day until the ear lobe heals, in order to prevent the opening from being closed over with scar tissue. Girls wear earrings from the time they are only a few months old.

The religious part of the naming ceremony is usually attended only by men. Meanwhile, the wife is having her own reception in another part of the compound. Women flock in—for many of them, this is one of the rare occasions when they can leave their own compound. A few at a time are admitted to see the baby and greet the mother. From time to time, a woman will rise and loudly shout praises of the child and family, ending in the high nasal trill that is the Hausa woman's way of expressing joy at weddings and births.

Among the other ethnic groups living in Katsina, the seven-day waiting period before giving a name is also observed. The delay is possibly caused by knowledge of the high infant-mortality rate in Nigeria, by a desire to be sure the child is going to live before giving it a name.

Non-Muslim naming ceremonies are more social in nature—a gathering of friends. The guests sit in a circle in the courtyard, drinking beer or soft drinks. Cakes and meat are served, music is played, and a few people dance. Then the mother comes out and a few guests at a time go with her into her room to see the baby. A photographer is usually called in, and all the guests assemble around the mother and baby for a group photograph. Finally, the father stands up and announces the baby's name.

Babies in Katsina, as in the rest of Nigeria, are carried on the mother's back and breast-fed until they are two years old. A mother usually tries not to become pregnant again until the child is weaned, for, otherwise, the mother's milk supply lessens and the nursing child cannot get enough nourishment. Although a child is breast-fed until he is two, he begins to take other food at about seven months. This is usually a very thin gruel of millet porridge mixed with milk or water.

Throughout their first years, children may be sent to live with a variety of relatives and friends of the family. This is not an effort by the parents to rid themselves of the responsibility of caring for the child; rather, it is considered a generous offering of happiness to others. This is especially true of first-born children, since too much public pride in the first child is considered immodest and impolite in the smaller Hausa communities around Katsina. Thus, a first-born child in a village will often spend a great deal of his childhood away from home. In a city the size of Katsina, however, this practice is becoming less common.

Whether they stay at home with the parents or go to stay with relatives, children under the age of seven or eight are allowed quite a bit of freedom, although they do attend Koranic classes from the age of three or four. Girls receive some training in housework, sweeping a corner of the courtyard, perhaps, or carrying a jug of water from the well. Little boys may be taken with the father to the farm, if they can be trusted not to cause so much trouble as to offset the help they might give in planting or tending the fields. If the father is a craftsman, the boy is encouraged to watch him at work.

The child spends most of his time, however, with his mother or another woman relative. Since few Hausa women in Katsina have much Western education—a few years of primary school at the most—it is unlikely that the child receives much intellectual training of this kind in the home, although there may be much emphasis on Islamic learning. Thus, the child has difficulty adjusting to Western education when he goes to primary school.

Most children do learn to count—as evidenced by a number of counting games and the fact that very young children are entrusted with the task of selling peanuts or bean cakes, which requires basic counting as well as adding and subtracting to make change.

At about the age of seven, boys are circumcised. Circumcision is not the elaboratè ceremony or the symbol of initiation into manhood that it is in some other cultures. The operation is done by a barber that has been specially trained. As in the traditions surrounding childbirth, many of the traditions of circumcision indicate a basic knowledge of medical practice dating from early Arab contacts. The circumcision is done during the cold season—December and January—when there is less chance of infection. After the operation, the child is kept isolated until the wound heals. In order to prevent him from sleeping on his side, which might open up the wound, a guinea-corn stalk about a foot long is tied between his knees. Then, if he does turn on his side, his legs cannot come together and rub the wound. The pain caused by the sharp ends of the corn-stalk cutting into his legs soon makes him turn on his back again.

Sometime after a boy is circumcised, he begins full Koranic studies. This can last for several years. The length of time depends on the parents' ideas concerning the need for Western-style primary education for their children. The distrust of Western education is gradually disappearing, and a balance of Koranic studies and modern education is developing. Even so, children in Katsina and the rest of the north tend to start primary school much later than children in the southern states.

Girls may attend Koranic school, and they might also attend primary school. Their education is usually limited by traditional doubts about their intellectual abilities and by the fear that a girl who is more educated than her intended husband is not likely to have a contented marriage. In any case, much of a girl's education is devoted to housework.

Girls are married quite young in Katsina—thirteen or fourteen is an average age, while, in villages, the age might well be younger. Such marriages are arranged by the parents, although a certain amount of choice is usually allowed to the girl. Many reasons have been advanced for the early marriage age. The most common one is based on the traditional belief that women are by nature less pure and more easily swayed by temptation than men, and, if a girl remains unmarried long after puberty, the chances of her misbehaving and acquiring a poor reputation for herself increase. This attitude is probably the slowest to change in the Westernization of Hausa Nigeria.

In most households, depending on the wealth of the father and his adherence to traditional ways and beliefs, girls are put into purdah when they reach puberty. They have been allowed, however, to move freely about town before this and have thus attracted the notice of possible suitors. Very small girls in Katsina often wear make-up and jewelry, and much more money and effort is spent on keep-

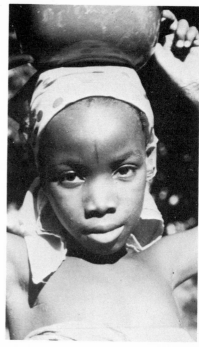

Young Hausa Girls

ing them well-dressed than is spent on boys.

It might seem that girls in Katsina enjoy little childhood in the sense that American children do, since early in life they are exhorted by parents to preserve their virtue, to behave themselves so that they may attract suitors. But for most girls, marriage is simply an extension of the sort of life they have been living at home. With polygamy and extended families, one woman is seldom burdened with too much housework. A young bride often takes her dolls and toys to her husband's home and spends part of her time playing in the compound with other young girls.

The marriage process is long and complicated, involving the entire families of the bride and groom. Usually the first steps are taken by a go-between, a friend of the man, who approaches the girl and speaks to her about the suitor. The girl can then either reject the whole idea or indicate that she is interested and the suitor would be welcome.

Then a series of visits begins, always heavily chaperoned by friends of both the girl and the man. The visits take place in the entrance hall of the girl's home. The girls sit on mats on one side of the room, and the boys sit on mats on the other side. At the end of each visit, the suitor leaves presents—money or perfume for the girl.

As long as his presents are accepted, the suitor can feel confident enough to progress to the next step. His parents contact the parents of the girl. The two fathers meet, and the man's parents give a sum of money—from one to five pounds—to the girl's parents. Acceptance of this token means an agreement that the marriage will take place once the bride price is settled.

After another interval—the courting visits can last for months or years—the two sets of parents set a date for the betrothal. The suitor prepares a box of presents for the girl

—blouses and wrappers, head scarves, cosmetics, perfume. Kola nuts, bitter nuts considered essential in any ceremony, are sent to the girl's family.

On the day of the betrothal, the father of the girl officially announces that he gives his daughter to the suitor for a certain sum (the dowry). The sum has been fixed in advance, and varies according to the beauty, strength, and virtue of the girl. After the betrothal, there is another waiting period of weeks or sometimes months, during which time the husband-to-be visits the girl each week, each time giving her presents. When the marriage date is set, more kola nuts are sent to the family of the bride, and still more are sent the day before the marriage. Once more, the groom fills a box with clothes, cosmetics, shoes, and perfume.

In the marriage ceremony, the groom's father, uncle, or some other representative formally asks the father of the bride for the girl and promises that the groom will take on all the responsibility of feeding and clothing her. The girl's father accepts the promise and gives the girl to the groom. Then prayers are said, and the couple is officially married.

The bride is dressed in a long white dress. When her head and face are covered, she is accompanied by her friends to the house of the groom. For several days, she does nothing; her friends prepare the food and do the other chores around the house. The bride remains in her wedding dress.

Meanwhile, the groom spends these days and nights at the home of friends, usually playing cards and gambling. After three or four days, the groom's friends accompany him to his house, where the bride is sitting alone, with her head and face covered. She says nothing, while the groom's friends try to make her speak or laugh by telling jokes and stories. She does not succumb. Then the friends offer her

Drummers and Women Carrying Bridal Gifts on Their Way to a Wedding

money to induce her to speak. She shakes her head at each sum offered until she is satisfied and nods assents. After the sum has been paid, she speaks, and friendly conversation ensues for a little while. When the friends turn to leave, the groom makes a token effort to go with them, but they shut the door before he can get out, and he spends his first night with his wife.

During the several days between the marriage and its consummation, the family of the bride brings sacks of food —rice, guinea corn, oil, salt, beans, and spices—to the home of the groom. The bride's room is furnished with a bed or sleeping mat and a great mass of calabashes and enamelware pots and plates. Thus, the expense of the marriage is not really all put upon the groom and his family.

Even with formal arrangements between families, marriages can run into complications. Before a girl reaches puberty, the father has complete control over her marriage possibilities, but, after puberty, she has more to say in the matter, and the ultimate decision rests with her mother. The father still exerts great influence, however.

In one case, Abu, a young man employed as a cook for an expatriate family in Katsina, wanted to marry a girl from his village. He approached the girl in the usual manner and was accepted by her. The father set a bride price of forty pounds, which the young man paid. The weekly courting visits continued for several months. During this time, although the official betrothal precluded any other suitors, the girl's father decided he favored another man, a farmer of the village who owned land. The mother continued to favor Abu.

When the time came to set the date for the wedding, the father refused to allow the daughter to marry. The case was taken to the Magagin Gari. He declared that the will of the mother must be obeyed and that the girl should marry Abu.

A date was then set, and the mother's brother agreed to act as representative for the girl, because her father refused to give her away. But, when the brother came to collect the bride, her father knocked him down. Then the girl, possibly fearing her father, possibly changing her mind about her affections, said that she would not marry Abu. The Magagin Gari once more had to step into the case, and sent the matter to the local courts so that the jilted bridegroom could at least retrieve part of the money he had spent wooing the girl.

Occasionally, a father will have different feelings about the marriage of his daughter. There is an old custom called *sadaka* (charity), in which a father may present his daughter to a *malami* or poor man, without receiving any bride price or courtship gifts. It is clear that this presents an opportunity of taking care of an ugly or otherwise undesirable daughter and that pious motives might not always be behind a *sadaka* marriage.

Sometimes, a girl who has managed to get herself a reputation for immodest behavior in public and for being intimate with too many men will be married off by her parents to a man who would be otherwise unable to get a wife. In one case, a young girl was married to a much older man who suffered a stroke and walked with a pronounced limp. He was so unattractive that he had not been able to get a wife before he married this girl. It is predictable that sooner or later the girl will run away. But, for the time being, she seems very happy. A young man asked about this explained: The husband has bought very powerful wife-keeping charms. Even though he is skinny and crippled, his wife is content because of the strength of his medicine. This the young man says with just a bit of an envious look.

In another case, a girl was friendly with several prostitutes in town and was rapidly following in their ways. When she heard, however, that an older man of the town was seriously interested in marrying her, her whole manner and appearance changed. She tied her wrapper more modestly and wore blouses instead of tight jerseys, and she toned down her way of walking and talking. Even among arranged marriages, there is considerable leeway for personal choice.

Divorce, however, is quite common among the Hausa. It, too, is covered by traditional Muslim law. When a husband decides to divorce his wife, he can merely send her home with a letter stating that he has divorced her. She can take this letter to a court to be endorsed. By divorcing his wife, the man forfeits the bride price and any money he had given as presents to her during the courtship. He must also pay back any money she has given him during the marriage.

If a woman decides to divorce her husband, she must go to a court, pay about a pound in court fees, and have a summons served to her husband. The husband may then ask for more time in which he tries to persuade his wife to return to him. If he is unsuccessful, the divorce is decreed.

No matter who procures the divorce, the woman must go through a three-month waiting period during which no suitors are allowed to approach her, but her husband can try to regain her, or she can try to win back her husband. If the couple decides to rejoin, no marriage ceremony is required. If a man has divorced the same wife three times, however, he cannot remarry her until she has married someone else, been widowed or divorced, and gone through the proper waiting period.

The high divorce rate is one consequence of marriages that are arranged and sometimes forced. Another is that the girls sometimes run away from home to escape unwanted husbands. Katsina has a large population of unmarried women, most of whom are young girls trying to escape a forced marriage. The Hausa-Muslim social structure does not have a place for young, unmarried women, except as prostitutes. This is gradually changing with increased Western-style education, and eventually women will probably be allowed to hold positions as teachers, nurses, or shop clerks without objections from their families.

The practice of arranging marriages strikes the Western mind as somehow repugnant—and, indeed, it is an unsatisfactory system if the marriage is forced without any regard for the wishes of the girl. The high divorce rate cannot be held as sufficient evidence of its undesirability, though: American marriages, contracted on the whim of the two people directly involved, have produced an even higher divorce rate.

Polygamy is another custom of the Hausa that seems

exotic to many Westerners. Many people, in fact, are surprised when educated, Westernized Hausa men have two or more wives. Polygamy is, however, a very practical approach to a mainly rural life. Wives produce children, and both wives and children can work on the farm.

Islam strictly limits the number of wives to four, and sets conditions that the husband be able to support all wives and to treat them all equally. Since polygamy is the norm, all people concerned accept it as quite natural. Co-wives usually get along quite amiably, sharing work and companionship.

From birth, then, a person's role in life is highly prescribed. There are rigid restrictions of sex; women are simply not allowed to have certain occupations, and, indeed, few would think of attempting to become, for instance, a service station attendant—a common sight in southern Nigeria.

The early years of childhood are given over to a largely traditional upbringing, and children are usually trained, by imitation, to follow in the footsteps of their parents. On the surface, little attention is paid to children. At any time of the day, dozens can be seen wandering about town, pushing their hoops with sticks, pulling their cornstalks cars, peering curiously at strangers. Many are selling something from a head tray, some will ask for a penny, whether actually begging or just engaging in conversation.

No child, however, can move through his world without learning. One cannot say that the children wandering about the market, hanging around the gas stations, or climbing trees by the school football field are not learning something. They are insatiably curious about anything that happens around them and are absorbing the traditions and culture of their people.

On the one hand, they are steeped in traditional culture

by their parents, the Koranic school, and the constant example of elders; on the other hand, these children are absorbing the slow Westernization of Katsina. They cheer the Emir as he rides by on horseback on Sallah days; they cheer him as he drives past in his big, red car. They see houses constructed of mud bricks in the old way; they watch the gas station being built of cement blocks. They are apprenticed in the trades of their fathers, but they know that they might become salesmen, clerks, or mechanics; that they might leave Katsina, posted to another city; that they might win a motorbike in a contest; and that the world beyond Katsina is open to them.

The people of Katsina have also to face the universal requirement of disposing of the dead. Their funerals are not the elaborate and emotional affairs they are in America. The deceased is carefully washed according to Muslim ritual. A friend or relative does the washing, women washing women, men washing men. The body is then dressed, usually in a long, white gown and covered with a white cloth. It is then wrapped in a blanket and carried to the burial ground.

In the villages, the burial place might be a special corner of the compound. The Emir's father is buried in a garden within the palace. There is no special attachment or sentiment connected with the choice of burial place. If someone dies away from home, he is buried in that place. This is based partly on the practical consideration that, in a tropical climate, one cannot wait too long before burying the dead.

There are several graveyards in Katsina, a rather new one near the hospital and another one on the other side of town, where the grave of Dan Marina lies. The gravediggers dig the hole a little bit longer than the corpse and about a foot and one-half deep. At the bottom of this hole is another one exactly the length of the body, about a foot wide and again about a foot and one-half deep. The body is laid on its side, in this inner hole, with the face turned toward the east. The Imam, who has accompanied the funeral party, recites prayers, with intervals during which the mourners silently repeat prescribed phrases from the Koran.

The body is then covered with pieces of broken pots, and the soil taken from the grave is mixed with water to make mud. The grave is then covered with this mud. A mound about a foot high is made. Some wealthier families will have this mound covered with cement, but this is the only marker placed over the grave.

8

Education

THERE IS A TAMARIND TREE on the market road, across from the graveyard, and every morning an old *malami* and his young pupils sit in its shade. There are ten boys in this school, young and wide-eyed. They hold their wooden tablets carefully, and, tongues between teeth, carefully copy verses of the Koran. When the passage is copied, they will read it off, all of them at once, singsonging the Arabic words as loudly as they can. If one of them fails to speak with the others, the *malami* will come and beat him with a switch. If the student's mind goes blank, and he cannot remember the memorized verse or read the lines written on his tablet, he tries to hide his ignorance by shouting another verse or whatever words come to his mind. But the *malami*, circulating among the boys sitting on the ground, soon detects such faking.

A Koranic School Alongside the Market Road

There are two systems of Koranic education: the Fulani and Bornu. The Fulani system requires that the Koran be read and learned, but only part committed to memory. The rest of the time is spent learning Arabic grammar and reading Arab literature. The Bornu system emphasizes the memorization of the Koran, so that a successful student can recite the entire book or quote any passage.

While they are studying the Koran, boys from outlying villages will leave their parents and go to live with the *malami*. During this time, much of their support comes from begging, and it is the duty of all Muslims to contribute to the support of Koranic scholars by giving alms.

Classes are held three times a day, every day except Thursday and Friday: after the early morning prayers, after the afternoon prayers, and after the dusk prayers. A big fire is built in the evening, and the children sit around it, chorusing the verses they are learning. Thursday and Friday are holidays, because Thursday is the day Muhammad fled from Mecca and Friday is the day he arrived in Medina.

The Koranic schools have been conducted in this way for centuries. In the thirteenth century, when Katsina inherited the academic reputation of the Songhai Empire, the city developed a pride in scholarship that is still evident. But the Hausa in Katsina have clung strongly to the traditional forms of education. In the beginning of the colonial period, Western-style schools were suspected of being traps to lure children away from Islam to Christianity. Since most of the first Western schools in Nigeria were in fact founded by missionaries, perhaps these suspicions were not unfounded. But by clinging to the traditional forms of scholarship, Katsina and most of the north lost ground to the other regions of the country, which were preparing their young men and women to run a Westernized Nigeria.

It was partly to remedy this situation that the first Katsina Teachers' Training College was founded in 1921. It was recognized that some Western education—in English, mathematics, and so forth—would be necessary, and, if the missionary teachers were unacceptable, the Muslim Hausa would have to produce their own teachers.

The old buildings still stand, although the actual school was moved to Kaduna and then to Zaria, where it is now the Federal Training College. There is now another training college in Katsina, located near the old one, but it is not a direct continuation of the former one, nor does it attract the caliber of students its predecessor did.

The buildings of the old Katsina Training College, which are preserved as a museum and monument, follow the architectural style of the north. The walls are of mud brick, high and thick. The windows, themselves a concession to the needs of the students—for most Hausa houses have no

The Old Katsina Training College

windows—are small. The roof is flat, and steps lead up to it from either side of the main gate. It is now a favorite gathering spot in the cool evenings for students from the Katsina Training College and Government Secondary School and for boys from town. The buildings are no longer used for anything, except to show to visitors. Eventually, interest in them will die, and they will slowly crumble into dust, like the old administrators' houses outside town. By that time, Katsina may be a bustling modern city, with traditional studies only a minor part of the students' concerns.

A totally modern Katsina is a long way off, however. Serious problems face education in Katsina—problems that seem to generate one another in a vicious circle.

First, a balance must be found between the Koranic schools and modern education. Those students who go on to primary school and beyond are quite old by the time they finish their studies, because of the years spent in Islamic studies. They are strongly tempted to cut their education short and begin earning a living. Beginning eleven years of school—six in the primary school and five in most secondary schools—at the age of nine or ten, means that a student will be twenty or over when he finishes. Primary schools are free, but secondary schools require fees, so that parents must continue to support a son long past the age when they themselves were contributing to the support of their own parents. To help alleviate parental pressure to quit school, the government supplies scholarships and travel and pocket money.

Financial support given to the students does little, however, to improve the quality of the education they receive. Primary schools are understaffed, and the staff they do have is poorly trained. After primary school, the better students go to high school. The less industrious students go to teachers' training colleges where they work toward a primary teaching certificate. Those students who cannot get into high schools or training colleges, or who do not want this sort of education, go to technical colleges or trade schools. Many do not go to any secondary school at all; many do not finish primary school. Some children still do not enter primary school.

The quality of the students entering secondary school in Katsina reflects the quality of the primary schools in the city and in the villages nearby. The quality of the graduates turned out by the secondary schools can only improve when the primary schools improve, for the basic knowledge of English, mathematics, reading, geography, and so forth, and the patterns of thought are already set by the time a child finishes primary school.

But the shortage of teachers is so acute that anyone who wants to teach is hired—whether or not he has passed the examinations for a certificate, completed five years at the training college, or even attended the training college. The theory is that someone is better than no one.

Thus, classes often will be conducted in Hausa, with no English used or taught at all. The teaching methods often imitate the teaching methods of the Islamic schools, with students all chanting out loud, reading from a primer, or reciting multiplication tables.

Education is considered a good thing. But it is not considered, as it is in Western countries and some other parts of Nigeria, a tool of social mobility. This idea is only gradually taking hold. Children in Katsina are expected to continue in the paths their fathers have taken, varying slightly, perhaps, but staying in the same general area. If a boy is the son of an educated man, he considers himself an educated person, and goes to school because that is what an educated person does. He does not necessarily go to school to work and to learn. He already has his position in life.

Aside from the attitude of the students, the schools in Katsina suffer from other things—lack of textbooks, lack of a coordinated curriculum, and an extremely high turnover of staff. Students may have three or more teachers for one subject during a year. The secondary schools—the teachers' college, high school, and women's teachers' college, are staffed largely by expatriates: Peace Corps volunteers and Canadian, English, American, and Indian teachers on contract. The expatriates are usually on one- or two-year contracts and spend their first six months adjusting to the country and their last six months preparing to leave; they actually devote barely a year to serious, effective teaching. Well-qualified Nigerians usually want to advance to administrative posts, or are posted to other schools, apparently at the whim of the ministries.

With the high turnover of staff, the school administration

is faced with the problem of maintaining a unified curriculum. When individual teachers request textbooks, the text may easily change with each new teacher, and textbooks may arrive in the mail months after the teacher who had ordered them has left for Canada or Ceylon.

The educational system is nominally administered by the state Ministry of Education, and certification is based on standards used throughout English-speaking West Africa. But communication is slow between schools and ministries, and the whole situation can be chaotic and frustrating.

Attempts are now being made to develop a standard curriculum, based on the realities of life in West Africa. English and American textbooks contain hundreds of cultural items—from baseball games to parking meters—which put up unnecessary hurdles for Katsina students. While an African student should become, in some measure, a citizen of the world, familiar with the difference in culture and technology between Katsina and Kansas City, no one can be expected to work efficiently with a mathematics problem dealing with the number of doughnuts a doughnut machine produces in one hour if he has never seen a doughnut or a doughnut machine.

There is a strong, persistent attempt to develop the education of girls, despite the resistance to it by both the community and the girls themselves. No girls attend the secondary school, but there is a women's teachers' college about a mile outside the town walls. Teaching is one profession that is gradually being accepted for a woman. Many of the students, however, are not from Katsina, but from other parts of the state, and are neither Hausa nor Muslim.

At the women's college, the same problems exist as in the other schools. Added to these are the problems of keeping several hundred adolescent girls under controls that satisfy the moral standards of a strict Muslim society. A great deal of the staff's time seems to be taken up by chasing away boys, locking up the girls, and dealing with the girls' crushes on male teachers. These problems only lend fuel to the traditional argument that it is useless to educate women, that they should be kept at home pounding millet flour. But some prominent men are now coming to the realization that an educated mother helps produce an educated child.

Toys have been mentioned before. They are an important educational device, and Katsina children, in this respect, are somewhat more fortunate than Nigerian children in larger cities, for traditional toys, made from leftovers of the crops, are available to most children. In cities, where children must rely on more expensive, manufactured toys, they often do not have anything to play with, to help them develop manual dexterity and to aid them in creating imaginary situations in which to learn their culture through imitation. The little girl carrying a cornstalk doll tied to her back with her wrapper is imitating, and therefore learning, a whole chunk of the culture she will live in.

9

Agriculture

FARMING OF THE LAND around Katsina depends entirely upon the season. There are two seasons, the dry and the rainy. The rains begin around the middle of May and continue sporadically until September. From September on, the land around Katsina grows drier and drier, the grass disappearing, the ground turning from mud to baked clay to dust. In December, the harmattan, the cold wind from the Sahara, starts blowing, and through the middle of February, the mornings and evenings are cold and masked by a grey haze of dust. By March, the weather has changed—still dry, but hot. Even the early morning coolness is deceptive—it is already around 88° F., and, in the afternoons, the temperature rises to over 110° F.

Toward the middle of April, there is a day when sud-

denly everything feels different—even smells different. The
humidity has come back to the air. Encouraged by this tiny
bit of extra moisture, trees push out leaves and blossoms and
tiny blades of grass sprout. There may be no more progress
for weeks, though. Even the first rain, coming sometime in
May, does not really initiate the rainy season. It may rain
early, then not rain for two or three weeks. Seeds planted
can wither and die.

Everyone watches the sky. Some days there are clouds,
and in the late afternoon a cool wind sweeps across the
fields. It is raining somewhere. The wind carries with it
that peculiar odor of rain hitting hot dust. It rains on
Shinkeffi, or Modogi, or one of the other villages around.
Then one afternoon the clouds pile up and the wind does
not come. It is quiet in Katsina. Then the rain comes suddenly, pouring out of the sky, cold and wet and welcome.
But it is soon over, and the waiting starts again.

April and May are very risky months for farmers. The
success of the whole year depends on how they judge the
arrival of the rains. If they plant too early, the new plants
die before the full rains come; if they plant too late, the
rains will stop before the harvest is ripe.

In September and October, there is drumming almost all
the time in Katsina, accompanied by the wails of women.
Finally, the reason for the noise is seen. Everyone is in the
streets, praying for rain. Women dress in men's clothes and
walk through the town. The men form their own groups.
Even the Emir comes out and leads his people. The fields
bake in the sun. One more good rain—that is all they ask.
But, if rain comes, even a meager, insufficient shower, they
must stop praying. The season is over; they must harvest
what they can.

The main cash crop, or export crop, is peanuts. Thousands of tons are sent out of the north every year. Acres

and acres stretch out, marked by neat rows of little humps, little bushes with small dark-green leaves. Along the market road there are about a dozen cement structures: a cement floor about ten feet square, with approximately two-foot-high walls on three and one-half sides. During most of the year, they are simply convenient places for people to sit for a while on their way home from the market. During the harvest, however, they are peanut-weighing stations. Each little enclosure has a large red scale, and farmers bring their sacks of peanuts to be weighed and sold. In almost every farmer's compound, there is a peanut-shelling machine, a large hopper with a mesh bottom. There is a handle outside the hopper, which moves a bar of metal back and forth along this mesh, rubbing off the shells and forcing the peanuts through the screening.

Although peanuts are primarily for export, some are sold locally. They are as popular here as a snack as they are in America. Around town, little girls sell roasted nuts from head trays. The peanuts are also pounded into a paste—peanut butter, essentially—which is used to flavor meat stews. The principal use of peanuts in this region, as in the rest of the world, is as a source of oil. Some is extracted locally, more is produced in a factory in Kano, and much, of course, is processed overseas. The matter left over after the oil has been pressed out locally—in small mills in private compounds—is mixed with sugar to make a kind of candy.

From the weighing stations, the peanuts are taken to the depot outside the town walls. There the sacks are stacked in giant pyramids about one hundred feet high, to wait for the trucks that will carry them to the south and the port of Lagos. Set against the reddish brown dust of the landscape, under the glaring sun, the scene seems taken from ancient Egypt, with men carrying the brown burlap bags up the ramp made of other bags. These great piles stay in the depot for months, growing in size and number. When the rains come, they are covered by green canvas sheets until just before the next harvest. Then, the road beside them—the main road to Kano—is packed with trucks. The pyramids are dismantled, and the sacks of peanuts are loaded onto the truck beds. Within a few weeks, the new harvest begins to be piled where last year's crop had stood.

While peanuts are the export crop, the staple crops are guinea corn and millet. These are the principal starch foods of the Hausa diet, ground into flour and cooked into a porridge. Both plants resemble American corn, tall stalks with long, broad, dark green leaves. Millet grows on slender ears, usually less than an inch in diameter, and its kernels are fine, round seeds. Guinea corn grows in clusters, about the size of two fists put together. The kernels are larger than millet seeds.

The fields around Katsina contain, besides the three main crops, tomatoes, red peppers, onions, pumpkins, and cotton. Gardens produce lettuces, carrots, cabbages, cucumbers, and other vegetables destined for sale to expatriates. Orchards produce mangoes at the beginning of the rains, guavas toward the end of them, oranges, grapefruits, lemons, limes, and some pineapples. There are even some gardens in which grapes and strawberries are grown, although these are such luxuries that even well-paid expatriates only allow themselves a few mouthfuls a season.

Not all farms or all crops depend exclusively on the rains. In arid countries, systems of irrigation are developed early in the process of civilization. There are many wells—the locating and digging of wells are old arts among the Hausa. With an electric pump or a wind, water can be made to flow through carefully dug irrigation channels to keep garden plots green and healthy.

This is not done for the huge fields—there is not enough

water or power to irrigate them. But, for small gardens, this is the accepted practice. These gardens are models of neatness and are often maintained by the more well-to-do families. The Emir's garden in town—not the one within the palace but another one near the walls—is tended by prisoners from the Katsina jail. Outside of town, he has another farm, with mangoes almost too big to hold in one hand and Mecca cherries, of a dark bluish red, with a large pit, as well as small plots of green beans, strawberries, lettuces, glossy pepper plants, and cashew trees, which produce a comma-shaped nut that hangs from a yellow-pink shiny fruit, tasting a bit like an apple, but having an astringent juice that seems to dry up the tongue. The shell of the nut contains an acid that will scar the skin. Some girls use it to add to their facial marks.

Beyond the fields of millet is cassava, a treelike plant with bunches of leaves shaped like hands. Beneath the mounds of soil at each tree base, the large tubers grow—to be boiled and eaten plain or grated raw and mixed with hot water to make the pasty starch that is a staple of people throughout West Africa. Yam vines grow here, too, the earth hiding their giant, brown-skinned mass, sometimes eighteen inches long. They are not like American yams but are white inside and taste more like potatoes than anything else.

The farming tools are varied. Tractors are used sometimes, for the fields here are large and flat, with no thick bush to fight. More often a simple plow is used, and most of the time the soil is still turned over by hand with a short-handled hoe. It is then worked through with another kind of hoe, its blade fashioned of metal slats, so that the soil is sifted through. These are the basic tools of life in Katsina, essential for both farming and building.

The land, when the rains come, is rich and can yield good crops. As in other cultures, old customs are borne out by

modern science. For generations, farmers have planted peanuts between the rows of guinea corn—thus restoring
nitrates to the soil. Some modern chemical fertilizer is used,
but, more commonly, manure is put on the fields to enrich
them. With so many horses, donkeys, and sheep around,
there is a steady supply of fertilizer.

Crops are not the only products of Katsina agriculture.
As mentioned above, the Hausa keep many domestic animals. Most families have chickens, ducks, guinea fowl, perhaps even a few turkeys, goats, sheep, and a donkey for
carrying heavy loads or a horse for more elegant transporta-
tion. During most of the year, little care is exercised over
these animals. They are cut loose during the day to forage
for themselves. Everyone knows which goat belongs to
which family. During the growing season, goats and sheep
are penned up, and donkeys are made to wear rope muzzles
to prevent them from eating the crops.

At the veterinary office, these animals are looked after,
and their diseases and injuries are treated. This, like human
medical care in Katsina, is free of charge. Advice as to
proper diet for fattening rams, rabies shots for pets, lina-
ment for horses, worm medicine for sheep are dispensed to
the public. In addition to direct treatment of animals, the
veterinary office acts as distribution center for local dairy
products. The Fulani in and around Katsina are noted for
the milk and butter they produce from their mournful,
hump-backed cows. But the cows are not tested for tuberculosis, nor is the milk pasteurized.

The local veterinary officials have set up a dairy herd at
Runka, a town near Katsina (it happens to be an elephant
preserve as well as a dairy center) where the cows are
properly tested and the milk put in sterilized containers
and transported daily to Katsina. Butter is also made there,
a welcome development since butter is no longer imported.

The Katsina dairy project also makes ghee, liquified butter much used in Indian and Pakistani cooking. Although Indians and Pakistanis make up only a small percentage of the international community, ghee is used by other expatriates because it does not need refrigeration.

The office administers, in addition to the veterinary clinic and the dairy distribution center, an experimental station outside of town. There, large numbers of imported stock are raised, and experimentation is done with hybrids. The greatest success of this program has been the introduction of Rhode Island Red chickens to Katsina. The local chicken is a scrawny, nondescript bird, hardy enough to withstand the climate and a haphazard diet but generally unreliable in its egg production, stopping completely during the harmattan. They are also tough and unappetizing. The Rhode Island Red is one of the hardier of the American species and an extremely good egg-producer. Thousands of pure-bred Rhode Island Reds have been raised at the experimental station. When they are mature, they are sold to local farmers for ten shillings apiece—three times the normal selling price for local chickens. The exorbitantly high price is intended to discourage the farmer from putting the bird in the stewpot or selling it as food. The idea, of course, is that the chickens will set about producing hybrids with the local breeds. This has been so successful that almost every chicken seen in Katsina now shows strong evidence of Rhode Island lineage.

The same efforts are being made to improve sheep, goats, and cattle. The local cattle, ugly beasts, are well suited to the climate, with their humped backs and loose-hanging skin. Any time one goes out to the station, the dirt road leading to the farm buildings may be blocked by a herd of Cypriot goats or Merino sheep. Different mixtures of feed are tried at the station, and the results of these experiments distributed to farmers.

With few exceptions, the local diet is comprised of foods grown locally. Although the general level of income causes some shortage of protein and vitamins in the Katsina diet, in general it is fairly well balanced. The basis is usually millet porridge called *fura*. Rice, cassava, or yams may be substituted. The basic accompaniment is a stew made of tomatoes, peppers, onions, and some kind of meat, sometimes flavored with pounded pumpkin seeds or bitter leaves. Okra, wild spinach, and other vegetables, as well as many kinds of fruit, are eaten daily. Sugar cane is a favorite sweet, as is *halewa*, a kind of taffy made from locally grown sugar.

10

Health

THE ONE HOSPITAL in Katsina serves the entire province. The next one is about one hundred miles away. The Katsina hospital is a sprawling complex of buildings—the one thing it does not lack is land on which to build. The first building, near the entrance, contains the offices of the two doctors and the administration, as well as the nursing school. Past the gate is the outpatient clinic, one side for men, the other for women. In the same building is the pharmacy. To the left are the men's wards, the major and minor operating theaters, and the offices of the chief nursing staff. To the right is the laundry building, the laboratories and X-ray rooms, and the women's wards. As this inventory suggests, the Katsina hospital attempts to supply full medical services to the community. It attempts this in the face of tremendous obstacles.

The two doctors serve a city of about sixty thousand,

with a surrounding population at least as large as that of the town itself. The services given are completely free: drugs, medicine, laboratory tests, X rays, and hospitalization. The salaries of the doctors, nurses, technicians, and maintenance staff are all paid by government funds. This brings medical services within reach of people who could not possibly afford them otherwise, but it also makes the hospital dependent on the limited resources of a developing country and at the mercy of bureaucratic inefficiency.

With a limited staff—two doctors and not enough nurses —medical care is severely restricted, but the hospital services are restricted even more severely because of the unstable water supply. Because of pump breakdowns, water is usually supplied only for a few hours, morning and evening; during the last part of the dry season, when the wells start going dry, water is in even shorter supply. (At all times, water must be boiled for safe drinking.) The electricity, too, fluctuates, and the town is subject to occasional power failures.

A typical day at the hospital begins at seven o'clock, when relatives of the patients' appear with food. There is no kitchen at the hospital, and food must be supplied privately. Little control can thus be kept over the diet of the patients. Often, relatives will ask to sleep on the floor beside the patient, or outside, on the verandah. Communication with the villages and even within Katsina depends primarily on messages sent in person, and families of people in the hospitals prefer to have someone close by to see what is happening to the patient.

A registered nurse and one or two student nurses are on duty in each ward. They perform the usual hospital routines—temperature-taking, record-keeping, and so forth. Around midmorning, one of the doctors makes the rounds of the wards.

A bed in the corner of Men's Ward One is screened off from view. In it lies a man who has had dysentery for seven months. He does not respond to any treatment; his case is hopeless. He is screened off because the sight of him would depress the other patients. While this man slowly dies, Mani sits on his bed and wonders how he is going to live. His arm has been cut off in a motor accident. Beside him lies Usman, a man from his compound, moaning softly. Usman has a high fever and has received two massive injections of chloroquine to combat malaria.

In the women's ward, the picture is much the same: fever, severed limbs, eyes bandaged after cataract operations. A young girl lies staring at nothing, thinking of the operation tomorrow. There is a lump inside her stomach, a lump she had thought for months was a baby. Now, this strange doctor will cut her open. For the third time that morning, she gets up and starts to go out the door of the ward. For the third time, the nurse stops her, a bit roughly, because the nurse is tired from all-night duty and her replacement is late.

The doctor is tired, too. He had been called in during the night when a truck, carrying twenty people, had overturned. By the time the casualties had been brought into the hospital, many of them had lost much blood. There was no blood bank, no blood with which to give them transfusions so they could live. How can one keep whole blood when the electricity may go off at any time—when the refrigerators may stop working and the shelves may become warm and putrid? It was already bad enough because the sterilizers often were not working because of lack of electricity. And the drugs spoiled.

The doctor let himself into his small office, nodding tiredly in answer to the greetings of people waiting for him. First came the student nurses. He liked to see them, for, generally they only had colds, stomach aches, or ankles sprained while playing soccer. Of course, they had already made diagnoses, according to whatever fascinating new disease they were studying. But he had done the same thing years ago in medical school in London.

An expatriate woman was waiting to see him, with a feverish baby. She would not say so, of course, but he knew she did not like the other doctor, the one who was supposed to treat "senior service"—the expatriates and the higher Nigerian officials. His colleague had become less and less interested in finding the correct diagnoses and had fallen into the habit of prescribing aspirin and chloroquine for nearly everything. Soon he would have to confront him, argue with him. But there was always the nagging thought that, after five years in this hospital, he, too, would feel the uselessness, would give up trying to identify the fevers and the pains, which could be cured only by drugs the hospital could not supply. Perhaps the feeling of futility would come after many Halimas, or Bintas, or any of the Katsina women who had decided to bring their sick children to the hospital had returned to the compound to have the grandmothers take over again—with the antibiotics thrown away —and feed the swollen babies some concoction of boiled leaves. When the babies die, it is the hospital's fault, of course.

But one cannot give up. Sometime, all this will change.

He washed his hands wearily and walked over to the outpatient clinic.

The women's side was packed and noisy. Children were everywhere, sick ones crying, and healthy ones, who had come with their sick mothers, racing around and shouting. Measles, chickenpox, infected cuts, vomiting, diarrhea, sore throats, runny eyes were abundant. The nurse in charge quickly diagnosed the obvious cases, scribbled on the record sheet, and sent them to the pharmacy. The next in line was called in: bleeding in the third month of pregnancy—dizzy, feverish, hearing ghosts of grandparents calling to her. "Go to the admitting office," he told her, but she would not stay in the hospital. She was afraid.

Sighing, the doctor went to the men's side. Here the line was shorter, quieter. Men are more reluctant than women to miss work to come to the hospital. More accidents here: a horsekeeper whose horse stepped on his foot, a farm boy who cut a finger off while clearing a field. A young man was complaining of lack of energy and very dark urine. Another case of hepatitis, now making ten in town—an epidemic starting. The man had a bandage on his hand. Yes, he had had a tetanus shot two weeks ago, after his donkey had bitten him, and, lurking on the needle, had been hepatitis virus. The hospital, which tries to cure, also infects.

On the walls were posters: "Clean your cooking pots." "Boil your drinking water." "Sleeping in crowded rooms can spread tuberculosis." They were tattered and faded, hardly noticed. Few of the patients could read English anyway.

It is hopeless, thought the doctor, sadness permanently printed on his kind, round face, despair in the droop of his walrus mustache. He washed his hands again after examining sores, probably syphilitic, on a man's abdomen. The water pressure was low. The pump must have broken down again. He went to the operating theater.

On the way, he looked at the clinic. He thought that, someday, one of them would die waiting—waiting to get a card, waiting to see the doctor, waiting to have a prescription filled, waiting for a nurse to administer injections.

In the pharmacy, all was chaos. At each dispensing window, patients thrust their cards at the overworked attendants. They supply their own bottles for liquid medicine;

they receive tablets wrapped in bits of newspaper. "One every day for twenty days"—a woman stared at the indecipherable script.

The doctor walked away. He knew all too well that she would take one tablet when she got home. When nothing happened, she would take two or three more the same day. When nothing but vague pains resulted, she would abandon the medicine. Hopeless!

At the operating theater, he scrubbed his hands again. The water pressure was almost zero. He called one of the maintenance men to make sure the drum outside was full. He glanced at his schedule: two appendectomies, a breast-tumor removal. It did not seem fair that cancer and heart disease, two great killers in the industrialized countries, should also affect these people, beset as they were by tropical diseases, by infections that were disappearing from developed countries, and by strength-sapping worms and parasites.

Walking into the operating room was like walking into the nineteenth century: tanks of ether, a leather-topped table, the old sterilizer. But, in it, he tried, and, for all its inadequacies, the hospital did save lives and alleviate suffering.

Tropical diseases may sound exotic and exciting, but, in reality, they are only varieties of ordinary human misery. Malaria, filaria, and schistosomiasis are all parasitic diseases. The last is not commonly contracted in Katsina except during the rains, since the vectors are snails and other small water animals. Filaria is introduced into the blood by certain flies and mosquitos. Malaria is carried by the female Anopheles mosquito. The symptoms of these diseases are so ordinary that many people neglect going to the hospital for treatment—lack of energy, headaches, body aches, fever. If left untreated, however, the parasites can settle in the liver or kidneys—indeed, in almost every organ of the body—causing serious damage. Other parasites include intestinal worms, such as tapeworm, so common that many primary schools regularly treat their children with worm medicine. The common use of human fertilizer helps keep spreading these parasites.

There are other unpleasant beasts: the tumbor fly, which lays its eggs on clothes hung out to dry, and whose larvae dig themselves little niches in one's skin. The first sign that they are there is a boil-like sore that does not respond to the usual treatment. The worms can be lured to the surface by blocking off air with petroleum jelly or an astringent; then they can be pulled out with tweezers. Or they can be left alone; they eventually will metamorphose into adult flies and go away of their own accord. Aside from the unpleasant feeling they give that one is moth-eaten, the flies are harmless.

More unpleasant is the blister beetle, a shiny greenish-gray insect, which causes no trouble until one brushes it off his arm or slaps it on his leg. Then it exudes a liquid that is extremely irritating to the skin and mucous membranes. The liquid raises blisters, which are both painful and itchy. If the blisters break, the liquid from inside them will spread the irritant.

These are minor ailments. More serious are the constant threats of epidemic—typhoid, polio, hepatitis, measles, and smallpox. Most Americans think of smallpox today in terms of a little scar a person needs when he is ready to enter public school or go abroad. One almost forgets that it is a disease. But, in Nigeria and the rest of Africa, it is still an active and dangerous enemy.

To combat smallpox throughout Africa, the U.S. Public Health Service, in collaboration with U.S. AID and the local ministries of health, is conducting a smallpox and measles eradiction campaign. The teams travel throughout Nigeria in large white trucks bearing the emblem of the smallpox eradication program. The teams consist of at least one qualified doctor and a number of trained technicians. The vaccinations are administered not by the old scratch method but by air pump guns that puncture the skin and inject the serum at the same time. If the lines move fast enough, one vaccinator can process hundreds of people in a few hours. The teams also carry measles vaccine, administered by air gun, and vaccinate all children under four years.

The team's move into Katsina was typical of the pattern established throughout West Africa. A preliminary trip is made, dates are set up, and local technicians are hired. When they return on the scheduled date, they are given an audience with the Emir. Photographers gather around, clicking away with their cameras, and the Emir rolls up the sleeve of his *riga* and allows himself to be the first one vaccinated in Katsina. Then his counselors and staff, the provincial secretary, and the district officer are also publicly vaccinated.

After this, the team sets up centers in the schools and in the market places, where people normally congregate and where there is enough space to handle the crowds. A count is kept and checked against census records, although the records are outdated.

The vaccination is painless—although some students come away claiming pain and stiffness enough to excuse them from classes for two days. Their complaints would be more convincing if they could consistently remember which arm had been vaccinated. Other people, finding it painless, use it as a kind of prestige. One gardener was vaccinated once at the school, once at the market, again at the mosque, and once again in his village a few miles from Katsina. This does not help the record-keeping. The smallpox eradication campaign is beginning, finally, to wipe the disease off the face of the earth.

Leprosy, however, is still a major problem. There are leprosariums and treatment centers throughout Nigeria. There is one just outside of Katsina. But little seems to be done, and the streets are filled with lepers begging—their hands and feet little more than stumps, their faces scarred and disfigured. Leprosy is a disease of Biblical times; it seems out of place in a world of jet planes and rockets to the moon. But Katsina is not yet truly part of that modern world, and leprosy is still an active and ugly reality.

Not all beggars are lepers. Blindness seems a particularly common affliction in Katsina. During the cold part of the dry season, the harmattan blows tons of dust across the land. During this time, everyone has colds, everyone is coughing, everyone's eyes are irritated. This irritation often leads to an infection, causing the eyes to water and itch or hurt. If started early enough, the treatment is quick and effective: antibiotic eye drops or ointment. If left untreated, blindness eventually will develop. Besides this dust-carried infection, common eye troubles are much more serious. There is no optometrist, no oculist. Only the rich wear properly fitted glasses, usually imported.

In America one seldom sees cripples. The victims of accidents or crippling diseases are usually outfitted with artificial limbs or with braces, and they receive physical and occupational therapy; although they may curse the cruelty of their fate, most are able to live something approaching a normal life.

On an average day in Katsina, one can encounter the entire spectrum of human misery: a man hobbling on a wooden leg—not a lifelike plastic and steel prosthesis, but a peg leg straight out of *Treasure Island;* a boy with a homemade wooden crutch, one of whose legs is twisted and withered. Most disturbing are the people who cannot walk, whose lives consist of getting from one place to another on their hands and knees—their useless feet waving in the air, sandals on their hands, and wooden blocks protecting their knees. They are the victims of polio, of birth defects, and of broken bones poorly mended. Until there are more than two doctors and more than a few dozen nurses; until there are trained therapists, clinics, supplies of orthopedic equipment; until people learn to trust these things and to use them if they are there—the presence of these people will remain an everyday tragedy on Katsina streets.

11

Local Crafts
and Industries

IT IS POSSIBLE to subsist entirely on the products of Katsina: to live in a house built of Katsina clay, to wear clothes woven and sewn in Katsina—from cotton grown in the fields around the town—to walk in shoes made of locally tanned leather. One can fetch water from the well in locally made pots, store it in special cooling pots, and drink it from clay or calabash cups. Millet and guinea corn from Katsina fields are pounded into flour in wooden mortars by the women and mixed with milk from Katsina in calabash bowls. The porridge is eaten with calabash spoons. Meat and pepper soup can be cooked in clay cooking pots. One sleeps on mats of Katsina straw.

Even when the raw material comes from outside Katsina, the ingenuity and craft of the local artisans can turn it into

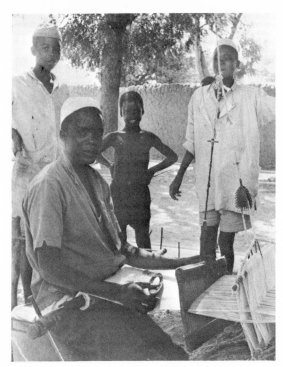

Weaving

something never imagined by the original supplier. Six-ounce evaporated-milk cans are transformed into kerosene lamps: Two holes are punched in each and a funnel is inserted in one hole, to fill the can with kerosene, and a small metal collar, which holds the wick, is inserted in the other. At the night market, no vendor is without several of these lamps.

Clothmaking is a major local craft. It is practiced exclusively by men and is considered a hobby. They sell the cloth, of course, but they do not consider the making of it to be a job.

The loom is very simple. The warp threads stretch out six feet or so in front of the seated weaver. They are tied to an old grinding stone with a hole cut in the middle. The warp threads pass through a frame, which keeps each neatly separated from the others. The weaver sets the pattern with two bamboo rods attached to foot pedals. As he presses down on one of the pedals, certain threads are depressed, and he passes the shuttle through them. The patterns are not simple or unsophisticated, but are often subtle plaids and checks. They are so sophisticated, in fact, that, having bought a piece of cloth and sewn it into a dress or skirt, a foreigner is unlikely to notice that it is a piece of hand-woven African cloth. The cloth that most non-Africans would identify as "really African" was probably woven and printed in Holland. The traditional color of most Katsina weaving was a deep indigo. Now, the weavers use threads dyed with modern, imported dyes, producing a wide range of colors.

The weaving is done in strips of either eight inches or thirty inches, depending on the technique preferred by the weaver. The strips are then sewn together to make a piece sufficient for a woman's dress or wrapper. Unfortunately, when sewn together, the plaids and stripes seldom fit together perfectly, making Western-style dressmaking difficult.

Over the loom is a ring with several small pieces of metal attached. This is connected to the foot pedals, and, while the weaver works the shuttle back and forth, the metal pieces tinkle merrily. One wonders what purpose this serves —until one realizes that its only purpose is to create noise. The weaver uses the rhythm of the metal bits to help keep his feet moving.

Few people wear hand-woven cloth anymore, and the weavers, as most practitioners of the old crafts, complain that, when they die, there will be no one to take their places. The same fate is even more imminent for the dyers. Only the people of the villages and the Tuareg now use indigo-dyed cloth. Most others prefer other colors and more dependable dyes. The dye pits in Katsina will probably be kept longer than those in other towns and may be preserved as a historical site even after they are no longer used, because, according to legend, Dan Marina, the Koranic scholar and poet, began his life at the dye pits.

Dye Pits

Katsina's dye pits are on Hanyar Gidan Yari, the road to the Yandaka gate. They are set back from the road, on higher ground. The pits themselves are six to nine feet deep. They are lined either with cement or with the sediment of indigo and wood ash. When the dye in the pit is "dead," when it will no longer color the threads dipped into it, it is scooped out, and the sediment is separated. It is mixed like clay and formed into balls. These are then burnt, and the ash mixed with water like cement. Formerly people used this sediment ash to cement their houses decoratively, but no one does this now.

The indigo comes from a locally grown plant, which is harvested during the rainy season. It is stacked in the fields and allowed to soak up the rain after it is cut. Fermentation then begins. When fermented to the proper degree—something determined not by dates but by expert smelling and touching—the plants are chopped up. The pit is filled with water, and wood ash and indigo leaves are added. After this has set for three days, burnt pit sediment is added. Then the mixture is stirred every two days for ten days. After this, the dyeing can begin.

If cloth or thread is left for a short time in the pit, it turns blue; if left for a longer period, it turns black. The degree of color is really of only minor importance, since the cloth will fade when it is washed. When already woven cloth is left for a long time in the pit, it dries to a very stiff finish. The dye often rubs off because the cloth has been supersaturated. The Tuareg, the chief users of the indigo cloth, have been called the blue men of the desert because of the blue sheen their faces acquire from their indigo turbans and veils.

Everything in Katsina goes by seasons. Dyeing begins at the end of the rainy season, when the indigo leaves have been properly fermented and the dye has been mixed. It ends toward the beginning of the next rainy season, when the supply of indigo has been exhausted and the first heavy rains of the season dilute the dye in the pits.

Building is also a dry-season activity. During the long, hot days of the dry season, the sun bakes the bricks until they are hard enough to withstand any thunderstorm. First, the mud must be dug to make the bricks. People near the edge of town at one time raided the walls for building mud, but the Emir called a halt to it. Now most mud is dug from several open pits scattered throughout the town. It is these pits that provide some of the most striking scenes in Katsina. One glances through an opening between compounds and sees the ravaged surface of the pit, the stark outline of houses on the horizon. In the flat, bleached light of a hot afternoon, it seems a landscape from another world.

The mud is transported from the pits to the building sites in the two-wheeled carts that transport nearly everything too heavy for a man to carry on his head. Each is a kind of oversized wheelbarrow, pushed or pulled by one to ten men, depending on the weight of the load. At the building site, the mud is dumped in a pile and mixed with enough chopped straw and water to make the right consistency for forming the bricks.

The mason and one or two apprentices set to work. A double handful of clay is grasped, weighed deftly with a little bouncing motion, rolled into a cylinder on the ground, set on end, and squashed down a little. In one motion, the mason turns from the finished brick to the pile of damp clay and begins the next one. Within a day, the building site is filled with rows of bricks, shaped like giant chocolate kisses, six inches in diameter at the base and eight inches in height.

Then the outline of the house is drawn on the ground and a shallow ditch dug along the line. A double row of bricks is set in the ditch; this forms the foundation. The spaces between the bricks and the top of the row are packed with mud so that no spaces show, and the top presents a level surface for the next layer of bricks. An apprentice will usually work first, putting the bricks in place, while the mason follows with a big basin of mud, filling in and

Mud Pits

smoothing over the wall. The operation is continued until the wall is about six feet high. If it is the room of a house, a space will be left open for the door. If it is the wall that surrounds a compound, it will usually be higher and thicker. The ideal height is one such that a man riding by on horseback cannot see into the compound.

When the wall has dried for a day or two, it is covered with an outer, decorative layer. This might be cement, but more usually is clay. The mason swirls his stroke as he smooths on the clay, producing a pleasant all-over pattern. Sometimes he goes further, and actually decorates the wall

A Roofmaker Delivering His Wares

with complicated, geometrical patterns, passages from the Koran, the date of building the house, and the owner's name. If the wall has been covered with cement, often it is whitewashed and the designs are put on with colored paint.

For the usual round, one-room house, another craftsman must be called: the roofer. He makes a conical straw roof. The framework is made from guinea-corn stalks, over which a thick layer of straw is lashed. It is common, during the dry season, to see a man walking quietly along the road with a straw roof balanced on his head like an oversized coolie hat.

If a mud roof is preferred, as it is by more well-to-do householders, a framework of wooden bars is attached to the walls. This is covered by straw mats and then plastered with mud.

Potmaking, too, is a dry-season activity. The earth around Katsina is red clay: Practically all one has to do is dig, and he has the material for any number of pots. A skilled potter can make vessels that serve most domestic needs—for cooking, water-carrying, water-cooling, millet-beer–making—and can also produce more Westernized objects—tea sets, candlesticks, vases.

The potter molds his pot on an old one, smoothing the clay up the sides, then cracking the mold pot and taking it out before forming the neck. Some skilled potters do not use a mold but, rather, form the clay with their hands, deftly spinning the mass around until it has been shaped into a perfectly round pot. The pots thus formed are allowed to dry in the sun for a few days. Then they are fired: They are set carefully in a pile. Then, straw and small kindling wood are packed around them. The whole pile is set afire, usually in the late afternoon, and the fire is allowed to burn itself out during the night. It depends on the skill and experience of the potter to know how much fuel to use in order to reach the desired finish for the pots. No glaze is used on Katsina pots; their characteristic, burnished copper finish is achieved by polishing them after they are fired.

Not only the shapes but also the materials used vary according to the purpose of the item being made. A cooking pot is rather thin, to transfer heat more quickly. A jug used to fetch water is thick, to give greater strength and durability. A storage pot, which also acts as a cooler for water, is made with a high proportion of fine sand mixed into the clay, so that the water will seep out very slowly, evaporating and thus cooling the water inside the jug. Pots

A Woman Carrying Pots to Market

for millet beer, *burukutu*, contain a special high-silicone sand, so that they cool the contents quickly.

Water that has cooled in a clay jug in the shadow of a thatched roof is very cool and delicious—better than water from a glass bottle in the refrigerator. When potters turn to Western items, however, they do not succeed as well. Hot tea or coffee from a locally made cup has a distinct earthy taste, not really unpleasant, but distracting.

On market day, men drive into town donkeys with great loads of pots lashed to their sides. Women come, bearing

A Leatherworker and Young Admirer

head carriers shaped like giant wheels, with a pot tied to each spoke. If she is not carrying a baby, a woman will often have a pot tied on her back as well.

The leatherworkers in Katsina can do almost anything that has to do with leather-making. They can make shoes and sandals and repair them, repair saddle gear, make reins and stirrup straps, and make belts of any description, as well as fashioning the odd item such as a harness and leash for a pet civet cat. The best leather-maker is an old man, living and working in a tiny shop. He has assistants but complains that none of them are really interested in continuing the finer work and that already he has degenerated into little more than a shoe-repairman.

Since several cows are killed every day in Katsina to provide meat for the market, there is no shortage of hides to be tanned. The cowhide is soaked overnight in a mixture of

Leather Sandals in the Market

water and wood ash. This softens the leather, although the odor after it has been soaking is almost unbearable. The hide is then stretched out, and the hair is scraped off with a flat, two-handled knife. The scraped hide is then soaked in a series of infusions of local plants to further the softening process and to remove the odor. Finally, it is placed in a mixture of herbs and the green sap of the tamarind fruit, and the leather turns from its natural brown to a dark red, which is the popular color for most articles. If black leather is preferred, it is dyed black after the tamarind treatment.

Leatherworkers make the pouches for *layas*, the amulets that nearly everyone wears, but they are not allowed to look at the charm itself, which is tightly wrapped in string and covered with a black powder, or to question what it is for. They only follow the instructions of the *malami* who brings them the charms to be covered.

Katsina is one of the few places left in the world where hand-worked leather is cheaper than the competing synthetic product and where the sophisticated segment of the people prefer plastic belts or shoes to leather. Besides making the traditional items, craftsmen also make decorative cushions, handbags, and suitcases. For centuries, much of the leather production of Katsina and Kano has been shipped north and sold as Moroccan leather.

Just as synthetic leathers are more expensive than the hand-worked real article, so ready-made clothes are more expensive than tailor-made clothes. The Hausa, both men and women, are fond of clothes and spend a large percentage of their earnings on them. Nearly every street in Katsina has several tailors, constantly turning out wearing apparel. These tailors do not use patterns but can either copy an article of clothing brought to them or closely approximate some item from a picture. These are the men who turn out the dapper Kano State suits and the elegant embroidered *rigas*. They do this on old treadle sewing machines, behind signs that advertise: "London Trained, Ladies and Gents Modern and Native Dresses."

Formerly, all metal work was locally produced: The iron, gold, and silver was either smelted in Katsina or melted down from bits of scrap. Now, many tools are bought ready-made, although many farmers still prefer traditional tools.

Cheap jewelry is abundant: Everyone wears the glass beads and gilt-painted earrings sold in the market. But nearly every woman has at least one pair of very good gold or silver earrings, and perhaps a necklace that she wears only on very special occasions. These are made by local goldsmiths and silversmiths.

In the old days, all the artisans of one craft lived in one section of town, and, to a large extent, the tradition has been carried on. That they do not cater to expatriates is evident; the silversmiths' shops are far back in a maze of compounds to one side of Hanyar Gidan Yari, the most active street in Katsina. The shops are small; the equipment is much the same in each of them. In one corner, there is evidence of fire, a small bellows, a crucible, an anvil, a tray with fine-pronged instruments, a box with lumps of silver, coins with the smiling face of M. Diori, the President of the Niger Republic. Nigeria makes no silver coins.

The silversmith lights the fire. A small boy pumps the bellows until the flame is glowing hot. The silversmith takes the crucible, a piece of metal, and a pair of tongs and holds the crucible in the flame until the silver begins to melt. Then he must work quickly. With one of his pronged tools, he picks up the lump of molten silver; with another, he draws it out to a fine wire. As it cools, he rolls it on the back of the anvil, smoothing it. He holds it in the flame again, snips off a bit, and, as it cools and hardens again, fashions it into the little question-mark loop that goes through the ear. Now he heats the lump again, pulling away a smaller lump, smoothes it into a ball on the anvil, heats it again, and attaches it to the loop. The whole action is repeated, and the pair of earring bases is ready.

Until now the work has been standard and routine. An apprentice could do it. But the artist in the silversmith is called forth to form the pendant part of the earring: a simple loop, a tear drop, the intricate northern knot, a flower, an abstract design. He heats the silver, works it, and cools it, while the little boy impassively pumps the bellows in the tiny workshop.

Ironworkers are seldom called upon to use artistic talent, but they use incredible ingenuity sometimes. For the most part, they make and repair farm tools—hoes, rakes, and plow blades. They also make all sorts of knives—butchers' knives that are strong enough to chop through beef bones, tanners' knives for scraping hides, leatherworkers' knives and awls, folding pocket knives, scissors—nearly every cutting tool that is used locally can be made locally. The ironworkers also work on consignment—a trowel for a lady from Iowa, braces for a bookcase, a chain for a swing or a monkey, a display stand for a wobbly statue.

Wherever the first ironsmiths of Katsina found their ore, whatever method they once used to refine it, now their descendants use a much richer supply: the debris of twentieth-century civilization. When the last reusable part has been stripped from a wrecked car, when broken hoes have been mended for the last time possible, when bits of piping, roofing, broken toys, old spoons, bent springs, tin cans, fish hooks, and paper clips have been discarded, the scraps end up in front of the blacksmith shop. They are beaten out, melted down, and shaped into knives and plowshares, hinges, and buckles.

Akin to the metalworkers are the mechanics, a new breed of craftsmen in Katsina. A car that breaks down in a small town in the United States means a stay of several days in the garage, and possibly sending to the factory for a spare part or two. In Nigeria, sending for a spare part means sending to England, Germany, or America—and waiting for months. So one improvises. Improvisation is especially necessary these days, because few cars are being imported into the country—there is a 100 per cent duty on them.

Few cars in Nigeria are in mint condition. The bad roads shake them apart. The heat and dust burn and erode them. The mechanics try to hold them together, and, for the most part, they do a remarkable job.

Several miles outside of town, a traveler noticed a peculiar scraping noise whenever he went over a bump. Upon investigation, he discovered that three of the four bolts that held the front axle to the frame of his car had been shaken loose. He cautiously limped into town.

The mechanic looked at the car, called to a horde of boys who are always hanging around his shop, and had the car bodily lifted onto blocks. He rummaged in a pile of used parts in a corner of his shop and came out with three bolts. Two were the right size, one was a fraction too big. Undaunted, he had one of his assistants start pumping the bellows by the fire in front of the shop. He heated and pounded the bolt until it was the right size. It was not, perhaps, as good a job as might have been done in an American garage with hydraulic lifts, acetylene welding torches, and a storeroom full of neatly labeled factory-issue spare parts. But the car was restored to running condition and was kept together until it could be sold several years later. It may still be held together by those improvised bolts.

Everyone in Katsina who owns a car has a favorite bush-mechanic story—worn-out rubber washers in the steering assembly replaced by a piece of old tire cut to size, gas-pedal springs welded back together in the middle of the night—semimiraculous patchings and wirings that keep a car running.

The mechanics, like all the other craftsmen in Katsina, learned their trade not through formal lessons but through apprenticeship. For the traditional crafts, the apprentice usually is a member of the artisan's family—a son or nephew. With the increasing independence of the young, however, crafts are dying out, and the artisans will accept an outsider who is interested in learning. But the mechanics, the new breed, do not have to look hard for apprentices. There is always a crowd of boys hanging around the shops, watching, trying to learn, eager to help with even menial tasks, happy to be allowed to hand wrenches to the mechanic. From such boys—with some primary school education, curiosity, ambition, ingenuity—will come the skilled workers in the factories of Nigeria's tomorrow. Unless Katsina can attract some of these factories, these boys will leave, drawn to the greater opportunities of the big cities.

Katsina seems reluctant to welcome factories and the strangers and foreigners they bring. Plans are made but seldom carried through. Katsina has no industry beyond the small crafts of its shops and workrooms. It is not a poor town; every year during the peanut-selling season, one can walk into the bank and see the clerk of a dealer sitting on the floor, tying up bundles of thousands of pound notes, and messengers bringing suitcases of money for deposit. But the city depends mostly on its major agricultural product and, to a much lesser extent, on cotton. The remainder of its fields are given over to subsistence farming. The rest of the economy consists of petty trade. Aside from the big farmers and shop-owners, the most affluent men in town are those who work as servants for expatriates.

This town, Katsina, with its flat-roofed mud houses, its streets filled with donkeys and goats and bicycles and hand carts, is self-sufficient. But Nigeria has the greatest potential for industrialization of any country in West Africa, and Katsina can either join it or fade away in the hot desert sun, dreaming of the past. It cannot hold on to political power in the twentieth-century with the economic power of the fourteenth century.

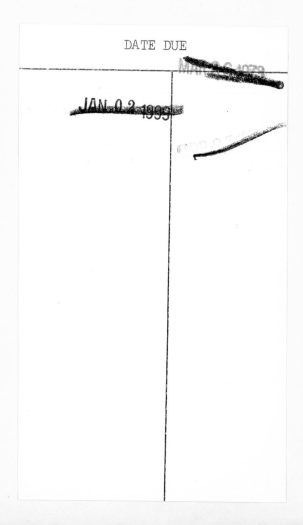